*A Gathering of Poets*

# A Gathering of Poets

*Edited by Maggie Anderson and Alex Gildzen*

*Raymond A. Craig, Associate Editor*

The Kent State University Press
Kent, Ohio, and London, England

© 1992 by The Kent State University Press, Kent, Ohio 44242
All rights reserved
Library of Congress Catalog Card Number 92-3198
ISBN 0-87338-474-1
ISBN 0-87338-468-7 (pbk.)
Manufactured in the United States of America

Due to the length of the permissions acknowledgments,
a continuation of the copyright page appears on pages 297–305.

Library of Congress Cataloging-in-Publication Data
A Gathering of poets / edited by Maggie Anderson and Alex Gildzen ;
Raymond A. Craig, associate editor.
    p.    cm.
Includes index.
ISBN 0-87338-474-1 (cloth : alk. paper) ∞
ISBN 0-87338-468-7 (pbk. : alk. paper) ∞
    1. American poetry—20th century. 2. Kent State University—Riot,
May 4, 1970—Poetry. 3. Protest poetry, American. I. Anderson,
Maggie. II. Gildzen, Alex. III. Craig, Raymond A.
PS615.G35  1992
811'.5408—dc20
                                                    92-3198
                                                    CIP

British Library Cataloging-in-Publication are available.

# Contents

## III

## IV

## VII

# VIII

# Introduction

How shall we gather what griefs destroy?
—*William Blake, "The Schoolboy"*

I

On the morning of May 4, 1970, two to three thousand people gathered on the Commons of Kent State University where National Guard units had been called on May 2 to help control student antiwar demonstrations. Students had been demonstrating for several days following President Richard Nixon's announcement of the escalation of the war in Southeast Asia into Cambodia. On campuses around the country, students had assembled to protest the escalation. At 9:00 A.M. on May 4, the Ohio Riot Act was read to those gathered on the Commons and tear gas was fired. When the crowd did not disperse, the Riot Act was read again at 11:00 A.M.

> Shortly after noon on May 4, 1970, on a grassy knoll beyond Taylor Hall and the Prentice Hall parking lot, a contingent of Ohio National Guardsmen opened fire for a period of thirteen seconds, striking thirteen Kent State University students, some of whom were nearby, others of whom were distant. Four students were killed, one was permanently paralyzed, and the others were wounded in varying degrees of severity.[1]

1. Official Catalog Statement, "May 4, 1970." Prepared by Glenn W. Frank, Geology; Thomas R. Hensley, Political Science; and Jerry M. Lewis, Sociology. For other information on the event, see "The May Fourth Site and Memorial" (1980; Kent, OH: Kent State University Printing Services, 1990).

1

Allison Krause, Jeffrey Miller, Sandra Scheuer, and William Schroeder were killed. Alan Canfora, John Cleary, Thomas Grace, Dean Kahler, Joseph Lewis, Donald MacKenzie, James Russell, Robert Stamps, and Douglas Wrentmore were wounded. A university ambulance moved through the campus making the following announcement over a public address system: "By order of President White, the University is closed. Students should pack their things and leave the campus as quickly as possible." By late afternoon, the county prosecutor had obtained an injunction closing the University indefinitely. Campus activities did not resume again until the summer session.

Within hours the shock waves were felt throughout the country and around the world. The announcement on the evening news was accompanied by what would become the signifying photograph of a young woman kneeling over the bleeding body of Jeffrey Miller. Student demonstrations and memorial services were held at universities all over the country in the next few days. Army and National Guard units were called into Washington as a huge crowd gathered for an antiwar demonstration on Saturday, May 9. On Sunday, May 10, Max Frankel wrote in the *New York Times:* "America was a nation in anguish last week, her population divided, her campuses closed, her capital confused, her President perplexed. The lines of conflict ran zigzag across the land."[2] Ten days after the shootings at Kent State, on May 14, 1970, two students were killed and eleven wounded when police shot into Alexander Hall, a women's dormitory on the campus of Jackson State College in Jackson, Mississippi.

The violence at Jackson State was not directly related to an antiwar demonstration, although the student government had organized a war protest a few days earlier. The tensions at Jackson State, a black college in the deep South, seemed to erupt more out of racial tensions and conflicts between students and local police that preceded the shootings on May 14:

> . . . almost precisely three years earlier students had clashed with police in an incident that broke out when

2. Max Frankel, "Nixon: He Faces a Divided, Anguished Nation," *New York Times,* 10 May 1970. Quoted by Scott Bills, ed., in *Kent State/May 4: Echoes Through a Decade* (Kent, OH: Kent State University Press, 1988), xi.

Jackson police came on campus in pursuit of a student who was alleged to have been speeding. Students at the time had seen the police intrusion as illustrative of the fact that the Jackson police did not respect the sovereignty of the campus security force. The violence of May, 1970, however, was not traceable to one single event.[3]

Shortly before midnight on May 13, someone set fire to a dump truck parked near the Jackson State campus. Highway patrolmen and Jackson police were called to the campus.

> A crowd of Blacks—students and non-students, men and women—had gathered . . . near the entrance at the southwest end of the dormitory. . . . The patrolmen stopped and faced Alexander. . . . Then without warning the scene exploded. Gunfire erupted, first in a sputter, then quickly in a deafening roar lasting a full thirty seconds. Students fled, stumbled and fell over one another, seeking cover.
> Then the guns were silent.[4]

Two black men were found dead after the firing stopped, Phillip L. Gibbs, a Jackson State College junior, and James Earl Green, a local high school senior. The state college board dismissed classes at Jackson State for the remainder of the semester and cancelled graduation ceremonies. By the end of May, over two hundred colleges and universities had closed, and students went on strike at over four hundred others.[5] The nation was facing the grim prospect that differences of opinion about the war in Southeast Asia had led us to killing our students in their schools.

---

3. *Augusta, Georgia and Jackson State University: Southern Episodes in a National Tragedy* (Southern Regional Council, Inc., Special Report, June 1970), 45.

4. Ibid., 48.

5. "Students Step Up Protests on War," *New York Times,* 9 May 1970.

3

In the years following the shootings, an annual Kent State University event called the Creative Arts Festival drew many poets to campus. Many may have come because of what had happened on May 4, 1970; however, poetry had been part of the fabric of Kent State for decades before the event that brought unwanted international attention. Although it may be impossible to determine when the first poetry reading took place on campus, William Butler Yeats read in 1932, Robert Frost in 1945, Langston Hughes in 1947. Some early members of the English faculty, including Arthur E. DuBois and Edward McGehee, published poetry. The English Department supported several student writing awards which were presented at an annual campus-wide Honors Day.

A campus literary magazine, *The Kent Quarterly,* was established in the fall of 1956 with poet Paul Zimmer on the board of editors and Carl Oglesby, one of the founders of Students for a Democratic Society and future compiler of *The New Left Reader,* listed as an editorial assistant.

In 1963, Jacob Leed joined the English faculty and energized local writers. Leed, who had published under the pseudonym Jacob Littitz in the *Black Mountain Review,* brought his friends Denise Levertov, Robert Creeley, and others to campus for readings, always followed by parties at his home down the street from where John Brown once had his tannery. Some of Leed's students began meeting in his office to share current work. In the spring of 1965 some of these students read in The Cellar, a small theater in the bowels of the Music and Speech Center. The Cellar readings continued for years and drew readers from across northern Ohio, including d. a. levy from Cleveland and Frank Polite from Youngstown.

Late in the 1960s, Dean Keller, a university librarian organized the special collections department at Kent. When university trustee Robert Baumgardner created the Robert L. Baumgardner, Jr., Memorial Collection of Contemporary Poetry in memory of his son, Keller and Jim Lowell of the Asphodel Book Shop in Cleveland collaborated to bring to the Kent State University library a major William Carlos Williams collection which included the manuscript of *Paterson,* Book I. Not long afterward the manuscript of Gary Snyder's translation of

Han-shan's *Cold Mountain Poems* was purchased.

The Creative Arts Festival, initiated in 1967, helped to establish Kent State University as a poetic center. Each year students brought artists to campus, including many poets, playwright Jean-Claude van Itallie, composer Karlheinz Stockhausen, filmmaker Samuel Fuller, and artist Robert Smithson, who created the earthwork "Partially Buried Woodshed" in January 1970. The new decade began with England's Eric Mottram joining the English faculty. John Ashbery read at Kent State in January 1970 and Gwendolyn Brooks in February. Then came May.

Many poets responded to the shootings at Kent State and Jackson State. Yevgeny Yevtushenko in the Soviet Union wrote a poem called "Flowers & Bullets." Lucille Clifton wrote "kent state." Denise Levertov's "The Day the Audience Walked Out on Me, and Why" was printed as one of the broadsides in a portfolio of prints and poems published to commemorate the opening of the new library in the same year as the shootings. Other poets who sent new work for the portfolio edited by Alex Gildzen were John Ashbery, James Bertolino, Gwendolyn Brooks, Steven Osterlund, and Gary Snyder.

In the coming years, the library's Department of Special Collections attracted national attention with its acquisition of a major cache of Hart Crane letters; the papers of James Broughton, Jean-Claude van Itallie, Cynthia Rylant, and Marc Kaminsky; and the archives of the regional literary magazines *American Weave* and *Toucan*. The department published books by Robert Duncan and John Taggart and broadsides by William Bronk and Tom Beckett. It hosted readings sponsored by the Friends of the Libraries as well as more unusual events like Jonathan Williams showing his slides of famous poets and Edward Field reminiscing about Alfred Chester.

Following 1970, poetic energy gathered throughout the Kent community. Ralph and Louise Shelly opened a used bookstore in Kent called Shelly's Book Bar, which attracted local poets who, beginning in the fall of 1973, came every Tuesday night "to proclaim, contest, and disseminate."[6] Emerging from the readings, Shelly's Press published chapbooks, broadsides, and *Shelly's,* a nationally distributed magazine first issued in October 1974 with sections guest-edited by Jack Ramey, Michael McCafferty, and Phillip St. Clair. In 1977, local

6. *Shelly's* 1 (October 1974), verso of front cover.

bars hosted Shelly's Press benefits that featured Paul Metcalf and band-on-the-rise DEVO. Also in 1977, the Shelly's Kent Area Poets became a nonprofit corporation and, under Jim Palmarini's leadership, began a poet-in-the-schools project.

Tom Beckett, whose *Mandala Book* was published by Shelly's Press in 1978, began his own Viscerally Press in 1978 but emerged as a national presence two years later when he and Earel Neikirk edited the first number of *The Difficulties.* One of the major outlets for language-centered poets, Beckett's magazine lasted for six issues.

In 1971, Robert Bertholf was hired as a new English faculty member "on the hill," as the Shelly's poets called the university. Bertholf was instrumental in the English Department hiring Edward Dorn for the 1972-73 school year and Robert Duncan for the fall of 1972. Bertholf taught the Black Mountain poets and featured many of them in his magazine *Credences,* initially issued in 1975. Through the Creative Arts Festival, Bertholf brought many poets to campus, including Joel Oppenheimer, Michael McClure, Richard Grossinger, and Allen Ginsberg, who sang Blake's "The Schoolboy" at the 1971 Festival and called it "appropriate for Kent State."[7]

At the beginning of the 1980s, regular readings were held at Captain Brady's (later Brady's Cafe) across the street from the original gateway to campus. Kelly Burgess, whose family owned the popular coffeehouse, suggested the readings, and the first featured Sam Reale and R. C. Wilson. Open readings were held the last Friday of each month throughout the decade. Although various people have coordinated the Brady readings, Maj Ragain has been a guiding spirit behind them for many years.

A frequent Brady reader, Ralph LaCharity, began a magazine in 1986 called *W'ORCs,* which was published at various moments in San Francisco, West Germany, and northeastern Ohio. In 1987 LaCharity and other *W'ORCs* contributors presented "April Aegis:Aloud Allowed," a four-day series of readings at the Brady, at several Kent bars, and on the city streets. The following year a similar event was staged, "April Ample:Aloud Allowed."

"On the hill" in 1983, Robert and Walter Wick endowed a poetry program in memory of their sons, who had been students at Kent State

7. Gordon Ball, ed., *Allen Verbatim: Lectures on Poetry, Politics, Consciousness by Allen Ginsberg* (New York: McGraw-Hill, 1974), 117.

6

University. The Stan and Tom Wick Poetry Awards provided for high school and undergraduate student poetry awards and scholarships, readings, and a proposed chapbook series. During the 1980s, the English Department Colloquium and Lecture Series and the University Libraries sponsored poetry readings by Jim Daniels, Patricia Dobler, Grace Paley, and Donald Hall. In 1989, Maggie Anderson joined the Kent State English faculty to teach poetry and creative writing. In October she and Maj Ragain met to discuss a Gathering of Poets to commemorate May 4, 1970.

## III

May 4, 1990, marked the twentieth anniversary of the shootings at Kent State and at Jackson State. One of the ancient functions of poetry is to remember and to heal. In that spirit, a group of seven Kent poets sent out a nationwide call for poets to come to Kent State on May 4, 1990, to remember. The primary organizers for the Gathering of Poets were Maggie Anderson, Ray Craig, Kathe Davis, Virginia Dunn, Tiff Holland, Judith Rachel Platz, and Maj Ragain. In addition, Andy Cohen worked with us from the beginning as a liaison between the Gathering of Poets and the other memorial events that were held that weekend. Alex Gildzen solicited work from many poets who had read at Kent during the previous two decades and acted as a liaison with the University Library's May 4 Collection. The organizers of the Gathering of Poets sought the support of the May 4 Twentieth Anniversary Commission and the Faculty Senate but felt also that there should be as much community involvement in the Gathering as possible. Many Kent residents helped with transportation, housing, music, taping, scheduling, advertising, and the dinner on Saturday May 5. As we set up readings, we attempted to divide the venues equally between indoor and outdoor sites, on and off campus.

In early January 1990 the call went out for poets "to gather on the Kent State University campus on May 4" and to be a part of the twentieth anniversary commemoration. We sent letters to many poets stating:

> We believe the presence of our nation's poets at this sad commemoration is crucial because of the remembering

7

and healing that poetry performs. We wish to remind the nation of the important link between poetry and political involvement in these times. We hope you will try to be with us to lend your voice and your pre-sence to our remembrance and that of the nation.[8]

We placed announcements in several national poetry magazines and distributed fliers at national conferences of poets and writers during the spring. In addition, we mailed letters to those we knew had written about the Kent State or the Jackson State shootings and to those whose work we knew to serve remembrance and political commitment. We attempted to contact a wide range of writers, and although our lists were primarily derived from those we knew personally and were necessarily partial, we tried to solicit involvement from different regions of the country and from different aesthetics.

The response to our call was immediate and overwhelmingly positive. We asked poets who could not make the trip to Kent to send something which might be read on their behalf, and by early March we had received responses from nearly everyone we had contacted personally and from many more who had seen our fliers and advertise-ments. Most of those responding planned to come to Kent; most who could not attend sent poems or messages. Nearly all of them wrote moving letters including their recollections of where they were on the day they heard about the shootings at Kent State. What happened at Kent State in 1970, and at Jackson State ten days later, was a national tragedy. By mid-April 1990, it had become clear to us that many, many poets remembered and wanted to come to the site of the Kent shootings to contribute to the healing, if not of the tragedy itself, of themselves and of the public and private griefs they had carried for twenty years.

By the end of April, we had a list of nearly one hundred poets who were coming to Kent from New York, California, Oregon, Texas, West Virginia, Washington, Arizona, Kansas, Michigan, Pennsylvania, and other states, and nearly two hundred more Ohio poets who were driving in for the weekend. We set up reading times for people who had only a

8. Letter from "A Gathering of Poets," January 1990. The text of this letter and subsequent correspondence are housed in the Kent State University Library's May 4 Collection.

limited time to be here, but many of the readings were open, in the Kent tradition. Readings began on Thursday, May 3, in Brady's Cafe. Open readings went on for several hours prior to the candlelight vigil held every year since 1970. In 1990, the vigil consisted of several thousand people who walked silently past the lights and cameras of the local and national media around the perimeter of the campus to the site of the shootings and the memorial to be dedicated the next day.[9] It was cold and rainy that night, yet at one point the number of the marchers was large enough that it circled the campus.

On Friday morning, May 4, it was still raining. Three or four thousand people, including those attending the Progressive Student Network's Kent State–Jackson State Commemorative Conference and those attending A Gathering of Poets, stood outside near the May 4 Memorial. Former senator George McGovern spoke, as did the governor of Ohio, Richard Celeste. The president of the university, Michael Schwartz, conducted the dedication ceremony. The afternoon speeches and poetry readings were moved inside to the Student Center because of the rain. There were readings and a welcome at Brady's Cafe in the late afternoon, and on Friday evening poets gathered in the Wright-Curtis Theatre on the campus to read from seven to midnight. From

9. In January 1970, Robert Smithson made "Partially Buried Woodshed" during the Creative Arts Festival. Sometime after the shootings, someone wrote "May 4 Kent 70" in bold white letters on the earthwork, making it the first, although always unofficial, memorial on campus. On May 4, 1971, B'nai B'rith Hillel dedicated a cast aluminum plaque with the names of the slain students and planted a tree adjacent to the Taylor Hall parking lot. In May 1973, the University Library established a May 4 Resource Center, which included framed broadsides by local poets in response to the shootings. In March 1978, the university's Board of Trustees commissioned George Segal to do a memorial sculpture. His work, "Abraham and Isaac: In Memory of May 4, 1970, Kent State University," was rejected as "inappropriate" by President Brage Golding and was later installed at Princeton University. In December 1983, the Board of Trustees established a May 4 Memorial Committee, which recommended that a permanent memorial be built. A national design competition, supported by funds from the National Endowment for the Arts, was conducted. Ian Taberner was announced as the winner in April 1986. Within days, Taberner, a Canadian citizen, was disqualified for violating competition rules restricting entrants to those holding American citizenship. In July, the Board of Trustees announced that the second-place design, by Bruno Ast and Thomas J. Rasmussen, would be the one to be constructed, and ground was broken for the May 4 Memorial on January 25, 1989.

midnight to dawn there were open readings at Brady's Cafe. Readings continued throughout the weekend, alternately in the Wright-Curtis Theatre and Brady's Cafe. The rain continued too and prevented us from meeting outside on the front campus on Saturday as we had planned. The weather broke on Sunday morning, May 6, and the weekend of readings concluded at Plum Creek Park with a potluck picnic and open readings all day.

Over three hundred poets came to Kent, Ohio, during that weekend. Some had been able to get funding from universities to attend; some were able to afford their own plane tickets; one got a plane ticket to Kent as a birthday present; and several came because eight or nine people who could not come took up a collection to send one from their part of the country. Poets came to Kent representing others, representing regions, representing a wide range of political and aesthetic perspectives. Even if there was much we might not have agreed about, we agreed about the importance of remembering this event.


IV


The Kent Gathering has already inspired similar Gatherings in Eugene, Oregon, in 1991 and in Pittsburgh, Pennsylvania, in 1992. The poems in this anthology have been selected from poems read at the Gathering of Poets in 1990. We see this anthology as a different kind of gathering. As you read it, it will not be May 4, 1970, or May 4, 1990. You will not be standing in the rain with thousands of others on the ground where students were shot. You will not be able to hear the actual voices of the poets who read here, nor the intensity and the conviction with which they read, hours and hours and hours of poems. You will, we hope, be able to discover some of the breadth and the scope of the poetry that was read during that weekend. It will not be easy reading. There are dark moments in this collection; there are also poems here that celebrate the act of gathering, poems that try to find a way to heal.

The editors chose one hundred forty-seven poems from one hundred thirty-one poets, and arranged the poems into sections that reflect the similar themes we identified. Section One includes poems that address background to the 1960s. Section Two is made up of poems about the 1960s. Section Three includes poems written in May

1970 and shortly thereafter, or poems written later about May 4, 1970. Section Four includes poems about related tragedies in other parts of the world. Section Five is composed of poems written for the memorial gathering in May 1990. The poems in Section Six are about children, often about the deaths of children. Section Seven poems speak to related issues of anger, pain, and grief. The poems in Section Eight address the importance of gatherings as a powerful political ritual for poets, and they suggest possible ways of healing.

Everyone who was involved with the Gathering of Poets in Kent on May 4–6, 1990, has already contributed in some way to this collection. All royalties from the book will be contributed to the scholarship fund of the Center for Peaceful Change at Kent State University and the Gibbs-Green Memorial Scholarship Fund at Jackson State University. We are grateful to those who came to Kent to remember, to the Kent community who welcomed them, and to those who have allowed their work to be used here.

*Maggie Anderson, Ray Craig, and Alex Gildzen*
*Kent, Ohio*
*November 1991*

*I*

Donald Hall

## *Tomorrow*

Although the car radio warned that
"war threatened" as "Europe mobilized,"
we set out for the World's Fair on the
last day of August, nineteen-thirty-
nine. My grandparents came visiting
from New Hampshire to Connecticut
once in three years; it wasn't easy
to find somebody to milk the cows,
to feed the hens and sheep:  Maybe that's
why we went ahead, with my father
driving down the new Merritt Parkway
towards Long Island. I was ten years old;
for months I had looked forward to this
trip to the Fair. Everywhere I looked
I saw the Trylon and Perisphere—
on ashtrays, billboards, and Dixie Cups;
in *Life*—:  those streamlined structures that stood
for The World of Tomorrow, when Dad
would autogyro to pick up Rick
and Judy from a school so modern
it resembled an Airstream Trailer.
As we drove home late at night—it was
already morning in Warsaw—I
tried not to let my eyes close. My dear
grandfather—wearing a suit instead
of overalls; my grandmother with
pearls from Newberry's—held my hand tight
in silence. Soon I would fall asleep
as we drove down the Parkway, but first
we stop-and-started through city blocks,
grave in the Pontiac heading north
toward Connecticut, past newsboys
hoarse, dark, and ragged, flapping papers
at the red lights of intersections.

15

Tom Crawford

## *The War Effort, 1943*

Everything right now is a reminder of the war I was too small to fly in:
green trees warming up in the wind, the bus driver on the corner, a
dead ringer for my Uncle Benny, Army Air Corps, eagle wings
clutching a white star flying out of the blue patch on his right shoulder,
lost over the Pacific, I imagined. The old ache in my palm for the
flyer's 45. Nights were dark. God wouldn't make my legs grow any
faster or give me a thin, brown mustache. You see, I loved America,
and wanted to come screaming out of the sun in more than balsa-wood
and rubber band. It was hard to throw myself into the radishes and the
potatoes, to believe in the dull earth—that a little green garden could
save us. All the color was gone out of the giant, oily carp I'd found,
dead, lying across from the Buick factory along the Flint River, so
close to where the night shift riveted together the bright fuselages. I
don't know why I had to find it or how my colorless uncle got so big
in my mind. He molested my little cousin and went, long ago, down
the dirty river. It's just that you make promises when you're a kid, to
eat everything, to the sidewalk up ahead that you're coming, by God.
Who can understand this country? The surplus of feelings. The peace
that never comes.

Patricia Dobler

## *Soldier Stories*

Great-uncle Alfred was pleased to ride
with the Hussars and fight for the Kaiser.
He liked the flashy uniform, he pierced
a gold ring through his ear for luck,
which failed him east of Budapest where trenches yawned
and stretched and swallowed him. Alfred spent
the next ten years in Grandma's house,
curled on a couch, dreaming bad dreams,
howling at night. Grandma warned the local girls
to stay away from her brother, so Alfred went back
to Hungary, brought home a village girl
and had a life of hitting both her and the bottle.

My German cousin Heinrich, on the other hand,
feigned madness in '44. He'd knock himself
so hard in the head he'd pass out
whenever an Offizier came by conscripting
fresh blood for the Russian front. Heinrich
kept falling to the ground, grunting and frothing,
and so he made it safely home to Osnabruck
where he shot dramatic photos of an Allied bomb attack
on the village church. He cropped and hung these pictures
in the pet shop he opened after the war, and he flew
an American flag to annoy the neighbors.

About my brother off the coast of Vietnam
there's nothing to tell, no tragedy or comic turn,
only a curtain he keeps pulled around those years
as if within that cubicle lay his own white-sheeted body.

Lynn Emanuel

## *The Planet Krypton*

Outside the window the McGill smelter sent
a red dust down on the smoking yards of copper,
on the railroad tracks' frayed ends disappearing
into the congestion of the afternoon. Ely lay dull

and scuffed: a miner's boot toe worn away and dim,
while my mother knelt before the Philco to coax
the detonation from the static. From the Las Vegas
Tonapah Artillery and Gunnery Range the sound

of the atom bomb came biting like a swarm
of bees. We sat in the hot Nevada dark, delighted,
when the switch was tripped and the bomb hoisted
up its silky, hooded, glittering, uncoiling length;

it hissed and spit, it sizzled like a poker in a toddy.
The bomb was no mind and all body; it sent a fiery
static down the spine. In the dark it glowed like the coils
of an electric stove. It stripped every leaf from every

branch until a willow by a creek was a bouquet
of switches resinous, naked, flexible and fine.
Bathed in the verdant light of KDWN, Las Vegas,
my crouched mother looked radioactive, swampy,

glaucous, like something from the Planet Krypton.
In the suave and brilliant wattage of the bomb, we were
not poor. In the atom's fizz and pop we heard possibility
uncorked. Taffeta wraps whispered on davenports.

A new planet bloomed above us and in its light
the stumps of cut pine gleamed like dinner plates.
The world was beginning all over again, fresh and hot,
and we could have anything we wanted.

*Ely, Nevada*
*1950*

Karl Patten

## *Saint Cow*

The hydrogen bomb they mistakenly
Dropped on Albuquerque in 1957
Raised no mushroom cloud
Over the white oaks of New Mexico.

    The poplars they atomized
    In '45 is another story.

This bomb only hollowed out
One big new crater
And killed one cow.

—How wrong to say *one*.

That soft cow, lazying in her field,
Settled down under her sun,
Milked and readying for milking,
Brown eyes thinking about
That greenish patch over there
And water in the old bathtub,
Always flicking away for now,
Never flicking away forever
Irky flies from her rear-end,
Chomping so easily her cud,
Broad mouth drooling,

    Is all of us.

I canonize her:  Saint Cow.
Martyr:  to the mistakes of those
Who do and know not what they do.
Feast day:  May 22.
Emblem:  five full teats.

Sandra Williams

## *Learning to Fish*

All afternoon we fish with Uncle George,
plucking from the waves
these ocean perch flying up on hooks
from froth and churn so flat
and fantastic—a bounty of unbounded luck.
Ecstatic with each fish, I wave and scream
above the wind that rocks our frail position
on this high-perched rock above the sea:
I've never picked such waters clean.

At home in his garage, George shows me
how a nail beside the gill
will help me to fillet. Sometimes I miss
and skewer the eye while he shuffles
back and forth on his bad hip
carrying meat so fresh
and smelling of the sea I think
I could eat it raw and glistening pink.

At night we share the meal—
George waddling stove to table
with our pan-fried catch;
he's greedier than all the rest
to taste what the Pacific gives
before emphysema hooks that final breath.

But then another lesson and the test:
"Good thing that bastard shot your Kennedy,
good thing he put a bullet through his head,"
and because I'm young, just turned twenty-one
and cannot understand his final feisty need
to fire debate, I take his bait
and shrill through one long run-on
before I hear the screen door slam

and find myself outside in the dark
brushing hot tears with the scales
still gleaming on my hands.

Deborah Pursifull

## *Blue Is for Fish*

Mother bakes angel food cakes
colored blue, lets me eat one piece,
then we do the twist. Her hips
move in and out like go-go girls.
My body won't go like that.
*Bring your thing around*, she cries.
Her arms whip above her head.
She bites her lip, a mother's mouth.
Oh Elvis, you killer.
The light outside dies to dusk.
Mother slows to a sway, eyes closed.
I close the curtains in the front room,
open the freezer, pull out
the cold square brown fish.
Night sniffs outside, I hear its nose
poking around in the leaves.
Or is it the old dog, hungry again?
Damned old dog barks at the light
falling in squares from the kitchen,
barks at the grasshoppers leaping.
The flowers are all closed up.
I hit the fish with a spoon, smack!
Mother is laughing again. Smack!
There goes the crazy dog around the house.
I hope she stops that soon.

Julie Fay

## *The Lilac Age*

All at once,
history was happening.
People shot lilacs
from cannons, from bows,
catapulted them.
Cruise lilacs zinged
over the landscape, a waxy
electricity. A woman was struck
dead in the center
of her forehead
by a clump of blossom.
Agent purple was invented
to foliate the hillsides.
A child was seen
running down the road
with a wad of it
on her back.
A man stuffed some
into a woman's mouth
to silence her
as six men fucked her
in a Boston bar
and everyone watched
and sang chummy songs.
A lonely man
in a hotel room held a blossom
to his throat, pulled it
from ear to ear.
The huge blossoms dumped
from bombers clog
chimneys, close down
airstrips, leave
interstates slippery
and everyone panics purply.

The smell alone can kill you.
In a matter of days
after exposure
skin bubbles, lungs purple.

Deep in the Mojave silence,
a bored guard little suspects.
Paid slightly more than minimum wage,
he blows dope all day, works
on jigsaw puzzles. On the horizon
like clouds, they percolate.
Beneath the earth purple cones pulse,
press in silos against the dead caliche:
Then it begins: one tiny blossom
drifts across his game board; he brushes
it away, casually. Then
another. He coils his forefinger,
flicks it. Before long,
like early snow, then
blizzardly, they charge
from all directions, mass-react,
each blossom splits
the next into this,
the lilac age.

William Matthews

## *Why We Are Truly a Nation*

Because we rage inside
the old boundaries,
like a young girl leaving the Church,
scared of her parents.

Because we all dream of saving
the shaggy, dung-caked buffalo,
shielding the herd with our bodies.

Because grief unites us,
like the locked antlers of moose
who die on their knees in pairs.

*II*

Christopher Howell

# *A Reminder to the Current President*

*for Lewis Cook, 1945-1969*

On an average afternoon men lay down
rifles, leaning into heat
from which a few will not rise
again. "It is because of shrapnel"
we say. "It is because of hatred
and ageless dispute and love
of country, which we have learned."
Though the cleanly young seem deathless
as this language passes over them,
neither the *zip* nor the sound of the plane
nor the singing wakes them.

On an average afternoon
by the trimmed shores, pacing, waiting
for news, the loved ones
approach the exact moment
which will not decode:  a projector runs
on and on in a dark theater
and the doors are locked. A drumroll
circles the drillfield. Carbines
sound once, twice, and again. Who
will cast dirt down into the cool rest
of itself? Why does the film go on
showing and showing these few gathered
in sunlight around a space so empty
only the earth can fill it?

Questions. We are advised to let them ride.
We are advised that life continues.
That, on an average afternoon, the mother
will be given medals and a speech.

31

That all of this will be long ago,
like an unused wisdom.

"God's flag is our flag," it says
in the handbooks. "Therefore, be comforted
and clean of conscience:  these deaths
are part of a plan." Meanwhile, the film
is rewinding; and the sound of a plane sails
the dimming heavens, far off, like a telegram
on its way.

Diane di Prima

## *Brief Wyoming Meditation*

I read
Sand Creek massacre:  White Antelope's scrotum
                        became tobacco pouch
for Colorado Volunteer;
I see
destitute prairie:  short spiny grass & dusty wind
& all for beef too expensive to eat;
I remember
at least two-thirds of you voted for madman Nixon
were glad to bomb the "gooks" in their steamy jungle
& I seek
    I seek
    I seek
the place where your nature meets mine,
        the place where we touch

        *nothing lasts long*
        *nothing*
                    *but earth*
        *& the mountains*

Judith Roche

## *Thunder After Thunder, Returning Like Rhyme*

It could have been called history.
It had all the marks:  blood on the walls,
steel shards blooming in flesh in riotous colors,
people marched blindfolded along a road
the feet didn't recognize, nowhere journey
usually ending at bloated river,
the earth scorched and the wells poisoned.

It could have been called theater,
with its classic theme of struggle against fate,
its medieval undertones of Passion Plays, Feasts of Fools,
fiery ritual of auto-da-fé,
echoed addition of the Inquisition,
its cadenced words soaring on wings of extremity
the gods would have appreciated
if they happened to be listening.

It could have been called nightmare
with its birth in stars and rusting memory,
shreds clinging to bone and promise of water
broken in the sour taste of the denouement,
coming, as it does, before and after and before
the silence and slow time circle
concealed in the half-smile.
Death itself instructs.

Lawrence Joseph

## *An Awful Lot Was Happening*

When you come down to particulars everything's more complicated.
Fervent gestures in the South U restaurant, even the Greeks
behind the counter listen. Burned draft cards,
lamb's blood poured over files at the downtown draft board
—acts of resistance, moral values begun.

Saint Augustine in *De Trinitate* didn't see memory structured
by public events. A great moment in my life—not purple clouds
which excited my longings in Nichols Arboretum;
instead, the rumor cancer spread through Lyndon Johnson's brain.
Saint Augustine in his *Enchiridion ad Laurentium* didn't see

her dress and bra across the only chair in my small room
at One Thousand Four Olivia. I couldn't comprehend
whether more words might mean more, my greed, untrained,
not yet certain of its justifications.
And there was war. And from the bluffs above the Huron River

rain of starlight above Ann Arbor's lights, three, four
bell chimes ringing in the Tower. It wasn't Rome.
She dizzied me with excessive desires and thoughts.
What I wanted from all my talk of beauty, she said, was power,
and because of it, she said, I'd cause much suffering.

Although I never bragged misery—maybe once. I was serious.
What was I supposed to do when I heard you could be beaten or
        worse
in the neighborhood in Detroit between Linwood and Dexter,
the color of your eyes wrong. These are facts.
Professor Fuller's response that no one taught them to be quiet.

Glass from the bank's large plated windows all over the street.
I telephoned—line busy; tried again a few minutes later
—no answer. Where is she?—the verge of tears.

Swinburnian dactyls merely went through my ears. Advocated
concision, spatial range, temporal disposition of simple language.

And didn't the spokesman for the Black Action Movement
also receive a number over three hundred in the draft lottery
and attend graduate school?—I came back.
Three years later, every space turned inside out.
January, noon, beams of light across you shake out. Confused,

whirling joy when you slid off me. I leaned
again to embrace you. Uniform Commercial Code on the table.
On the dresser, a cup of coffee, tulips in a vase.
How to explain to myself how much I love you.
In the Law Quadrangle—my peer. He commanded Marines

in the Anhoa Basin. What did I know—what hookworms are like.
What it's like to shoot a Viet Cong, popped from a hole, in the eye.
A piece of metal in your kidney. It's too easy
to be sheep, he concludes, softly. Or too difficult,
I add, softly. He stares at me and whispers something.

When I answered I intended to maintain freedom my brother was
        riled.
What, or who, collides in you beside whose body I sleep?
No work at Tool & Die, Motors, Transmission, or Tractor
while the price of American crude rises another dollar.
There really wasn't enough work anywhere. And there was war

God the spirit of holy tongues couldn't release me from,
or from my dumbness. Pressured—delirious—
from too much inductive thinking, I waited for
the image in whose presence the heart opens and opens
and lived to sleep well; of necessity assessed earth's profit

in green and red May twilight.—You came toward me
in your black skirt, white blouse rolled at the sleeves.
Anticipation of your eyes, your loose hair!
My elementary needs—to cohere, to control.
An awful lot was happening and I wanted more.

36

James Bertolino

## *Five Views of the New History*

### 1  Her Arms

He was killed
in Saigon

but not before he found
her graceful yellow thighs

were the forearms
of our lord.

### 2  The Marriage

No longer willingly
imprisoned

by the hypnosis
of the real

she entered the garden
of opposition

to be the marriage
of the lamb.

### 3  The Garden

Her garden,
terraced
to several heights of color,
was a congregation
of flowers

each bearing witness
to one of her deaths.

They found her late
in the bleached hours,
her face the salmon-pink
of the drooping rose.

## 4  Seventh Month

From deep in the crib her eyes
held him,
the long clear gaze
that said Father, I've much to tell you,
but moment by moment my memory leaves
and I still haven't learned
to speak.

## 5  The Face

Each day the face
of the savior we seek

seems more Asian
in the imagination—

the skin color rich, cheekbones
high, the feminine eyes

slanted deliciously.

## The American

You stand bent
before negation,
no way to straighten
your bones, no hope
of direction into death
or life. You fall

before negation,
and before you know
anything you rise
to stoop forward, to follow
the long reaching
of your shadow—

always before you.
However you turn
the dim light is behind.
You kneel, begging to find
a direction in dying,
to leave your shadow

for the light
of burning. You lie
before negation, you plead
for burning.

David Ignatow

## *Soldier*

In his hands the submachine gun is excited,
pouring its life out; he is detached,
searching for bodies. I am detached,
wondering whether to stuff and hang him
on my wall a trophy. From behind,
I could put a bullet through his head
and as he sinks, dropping his gun,
rip off his uniform, slice him down the middle,
pull out his liver, heart, spleen,
the whole works from head to bowels,
his brain poked out through his nostrils,
to keep his skull intact.
I'd leave in his eyes,
treat them chemically to last
for their lustrous quality.
I'd stuff with dried grass the cavities of his body
to achieve their natural proportions,
then glue him to the surface of a board
the length of his frame, hang him on the wall
in my study, the submachine stuck back
in his hands, his mouth straightened
in a killer's line, except
I lack his calculating way to do it,
and can only write to say
in any case
he is finished.

Vern Rutsala

## *The Silence*

Every day is a long pause without seams,
the world empty, winter everywhere,
cracked puddles like broken bowls
and the flat scuffed land

going in all directions on its belly.
Language gone featureless as numbers
one word is like another as a branch
stiff as bone scrapes its fingernail

across the kitchen window. After midnight now
I hear train whistles and braking wheels
that seem to carry sobs and wild lost
cries at the crossing up the street.

There is the squeal of slaughtered animals
and tires and the dead fields whispering:
curl up, a wind is coming; curl up, no one
will notice; curl up, the only way

to stay alive is to lie still as death.

*Ohio*
*Winter 1970*

Shinkichi Takahashi

## *Burning Oneself to Death*

That was the best moment of the monk's life.
Firm on a pile of firewood
With nothing more to say, hear, see,
Smoke wrapped him, his folded hands blazed.

There was nothing more to do, the end
Of everything. He remembered, as a cool breeze
Streamed through him, that one is always
In the same place, and that there is no time.

Suddenly a whirling mushroom cloud rose
Before his singed eyes, and he was a mass
Of flame. Globes, one after another, rolled out,
The delighted sparrows flew round like fire balls.

*translated by Lucien Stryk*

Bill Tremblay

## *Reverend*

*for Rev. Ronald Hardy*

You walk out the door.
The kitchen is still agitated
with the portraits of your assassinated heroes.

Soon the first snow will fall
or has fallen. Across the field
or down a rutted road
the lamp in the shed watches you.

Never before has gasoline smelled so intoxicating.

You are finally a torch
at the edge of your one lovely brook.
Black smoke billows off your chest
& a sudden gust of wind chews your ribs.
You have gone down in the grass chanting "Father, Father."

You have not come this far to tell your
self this. You run back toward the house,
beating the flames on your sides with your elbows
like a shaman celebrating birds
to press your cheek against your wife's belly
until your unborn child knows why,
gathering your requiem, your fellow ministers will say
your death was not political.

Yusef Komunyakaa

## *"You and I Are Disappearing"*

*—Björn Håkansson*

The cry I bring down from the hills
belongs to a girl still burning
inside my head. At daybreak
        she burns like a piece of paper.
She burns like foxfire
in a thigh-shaped valley.
A skirt of flames
dances around her
at dusk.
        We stand with our hands
hanging at our sides,
while she burns
        like a sack of dry ice.
She burns like oil on water.
She burns like a cattail torch
dipped in gasoline.
She glows like the fat tip
of a banker's cigar,
        silent as quicksilver.
A tiger under a rainbow
        at nightfall.
She burns like a shot glass of vodka.
She burns like a field of poppies
at the edge of a rain forest.
She rises like dragonsmoke
        to my nostrils.
She burns like a burning bush
driven by a godawful wind.

Sharon Doubiago

## from *Hard Country*

### Sometimes I Understand The Hatred Against Women

You are in conference.
You are planning the war.

I stand in the doorway.
I wait for the appropriate moment,
the moment of woman.

Then I bring you
my tray
of bread and meat.

You kill. And I always
look back into your body.
My mirror.

You lie dead in the street.
I stretch the full length of my body
onto you. I am crying

Let me couple with you still
Let me couple with you still

And the children I bring forth:

I issue to you
and the battlefield.

## Sleeping With The Enemy/I Don't Want To Talk About It

Like the legless, the armless, the sightless

it gets hard core

I mean, I don't want to talk about it, I mean
Mai Lai, was that it? I mean
level everyone, I mean

little kids come up to you
real sweet, you gotta kill them first
they might have bombs in their shirts

It gets hard core

You push the gooks out
at 500 feet
whether they talk or not

It's a bad thing to write about
It's a bad thing, you shouldn't do it,
*you know*, make it
marketable

like the legless, the armless, the sightless

I'm not going to say another word
about it, because, of course,
you follow orders

like killing everyone who wears glasses
because it means
they think

like my mad sergeant
who played Mozart every night
so the enemy would know

our location, he loved
the game

like shooting him in the back
when he and I
were the only survivors

like the first person I killed
a pregnant girl
I shot her in the belly
the foetus flew in my face
I've hated women ever since

it's a bad thing to write about

it gets hard core

like prostitutes who jammed
hair pins
into the ears of sleeping boys

like the boys who jammed
grenades
up the cunts
of the village girls

like frontier soldiers who scalped
the genitals of Indian women

and stretched them over saddle-bows
and stretched them over cavalry hats
while riding in the ranks

like being a girl in America
and watching the boy next door
leave for war

like the princess in the fairy tale
it gets hard core, you're

the property, the prize
your father the King gives away
to the warrior
who wins

like war and sex
like men and women
in our Kingdom, follow
the same order, domination
and submission, like war
over the land, like war
over the women,
the spoils, the prize, what's
taken

Like the 4000 member
CIA Killer Squad
Like plastic pellet bombs
that cannot penetrate
steel or rubber, only
human flesh, geared
to explode
at the height of the average Vietnamese

war is about our sex, war is the hatred
of the body, like

napalm, the fleshfire
that can't be put out

like a bomb called the Cheeseburger
like a bomb called the Nosebomb

like shooting your sergeant in the back

like CS gas:
you vomit to death

like weather modification

like the armless, the legless, the sightless
you
don't want to talk about it

Like the 22 year old woman
you force water down
then jump on her belly, you, the whole
squadron. You capture her 3 times.
3 times she escapes. Rests.
Comes back to the front, now

her misshapen body, her heels
you shaved off, the finger you plucked.
The color of her skin
is not a color. But you
are in her body now,
the fits she has
wherever she goes, what
you did to her
she repeats over and over
what you don't want to remember

*You can do anything to me.*
*I'll never talk. Free*
*my country*

like the legless, the armless, the sightless

like the bones of 4000 years of Vietnamese
who nourish the rice paddies
like the whole country
a sacred burial ground.

Sharon Olds

## *The Protestor*

*for Bob Stein*

We were driving north, through the snow, you said
you'd turned 21 during Vietnam, you were
1-A. The road curved
and curved back, the branches laden, you
said you'd decided not to go
to Canada. Which meant you'd decided to
go to jail, a slender guy of
21, which meant you'd decided to be
raped rather than to kill, if it was their
life or your ass, it was your ass.
We drove in silence, such soft snow
so heavy borne-down. That was how I'd come to
know I loved America—
when the men had to leave, they could never come back,
I looked and loved every American
needle on every American tree,
my soul was in it. But if I were taken and
used, taken and used, I think
my soul would die, I think I'd be easily broken,
the work of my life over. And you'd said
This is the work of my life, to say with my
body itself You fuckers you cannot
tell me who to kill. As if there were a
spirit free of the body, safe from it.
After a while you talked about your family,
not starting, as I had, with
husband and children, leaving everyone else out—
you started with your grandparents
and worked your way back, away from yourself,
deeper and deeper into Europe, the Torah
buried sometimes in the garden, sometimes
swallowed and carried in the ark of the body itself.

50

Jacob Leed

## *Two Poems Written in April, 1970*

I don't walk out much at night anymore
down over the bridge to town—
a bike backed to the curb at Al's Bar
a place I could get beat up in   I have long hair.

a six-year-old boy in the backseat of the car coming off Erie Street
                                        at the railroad station
saying tiredly out the window at everyone he passes bang bang

my mind my country beyond being lost
it's as if reading a few lines in somebody else's book
sets me off

threads. as ifs. blips.

I know what the minds around me are like, failing.

*

Back to somebody else's lines
out of stress worse than mine
he knows where he goes

down the peculiar coherence of his page
to a point somewhere beyond itself—
in this case an Ohio bar.

Over the pinball's bells I can hear a man
going fast in second gear against the longhairs—

a fanatic. But his ear's a fanatic too,
listening to a friend in a blue golf shirt
who tries to bring him part way back from where he's headed.

*III*

Alex Gildzen

## *Allison*

lured from corngreen commons
to gather lilacs & poppies
to stuff into gun barrels

but May had a darker meaning
& Allison of the flowers
fell on parking lot asphalt
her heart ripped apart

& what of spring?

rash volley of unreason
massacred spring

the commons where her kitten sprang
after butterflies
lies barren now

it's the winter of the generals
who would march us
over flowerless fields
to seek out foe   brother

it's the killing cold
of a world gone mad

still    the boot    the bayonet

*1970*

55

Joseph Hansen

## *To Jeffrey Miller*

*Killed at Kent State, May 4, 1970*

It is not easy to be young
but you won't fail
you can't fail now
you will be nothing
bones and grass
but you will be young
with your blood
spilling after you
forever
and all of us
washing it from our hands
every eternal morning
of your dying.

Mary M. Chadbourne

## *Enough*

Thirteen seconds for thirteen people.
It is enough. An index finger
in a fragment of a second
at the trigger, enough.

The bullets were sufficient cause, of course,
to do the work done, but insufficient reason
sent them out to do it. This puzzles,
maddens, wants sufficient explanation.

Think of this: the anonymity
of action in so brief a time.
It is what bullets make us,
faceless, no eye can follow
what was fired and say,
"This is mine." And so,
*"This* death *that* day is mine."

There is no ownership.

Imagine it this way:

>He pulls the trigger.
>The film stops.
>We are there beside him, to watch.
>Watch the bullet as it leaves the barrel,
>watch him, as he sees it stopped midair.
>His eyes transfixed on *his* bullet, suspended there.
>Laying down the gun, there is nothing else.
>Only this young man, this day, and his bullet,
>which he slowly walks beside, his hand
>cupped gently behind it, as if guiding,
>keeping it true.

He sees, we see, in this time-lapse,
the air split before its path. Up the hill
toward the crowd, it is infinitely slow
before him, his bullet. Together
moving toward a girl he does not know,
his bullet, his hand behind it, moving
toward the girl who does not know.

We look at him and feel
in the disarray of reason
that surrounds this hill
that it must be done this way,
of course, to know the effect
of your actions. To own
what you do. To feel beneath your hand
the warmth of someone as the bullet
goes in. And to stand there, stunned
in the collapse of her
in the sun.

That it is your work, that it is
no one else's, that you own forever
what you do—although they did not teach you
this—nonetheless, this is not anonymous.
This is death.
And you own it.

Sufficient cause
and insufficient reason.
And together, enough.

Donald Hassler

## *May 4, 1970*

We have wasted our lives as James Wright said
He did on bookish matters. We are lost
In John Barth's funhouse. Design of Robert Frost
Has been our creed, and now four kids are dead.
We talk too much. Our wives have learned to dread
The nights of mental exercise. The cost
May be too great as wrinkled sheets are tossed
Away for waste, and now four kids are dead.
But what else could we do?  The sonnet form
Won't let us drive our horses roughly shod
Or bull our way through virgin fields of hay.
Analysis is all that we can lay
Against the darkness and an absent God.
We save what we can in a wasting storm.

John Perreault

## *Kent State*

Although I was elsewhere
I could not believe what was happening
—the little puffs of smoke,
the pandemonium.

I stuck a flower in your gun.

And one would have been a mother
of three bright children.
And one a highly educated carpenter
(she would have built her own house).
And one would have been
a lawyer who cooked.
And one would have been a musician.

What kind of flower?

The error—only one of many
—was this:
to believe in free speech.
But maybe the error was trust.

Some of the children trusted
democracy;
some of them their commanders.

I stuck a flower in your gun.

I pulled the trigger
because I was told to
and I still see them falling,
here at the plant,
or in lonely corridors
at the mall.

I pulled the trigger
because I
because
because I don't know why.
There was another finger
inside my finger
connected by wires
to the President of the United States.

I pulled the trigger
like I was hunting.
There goes a rabbit. Bam.
And I eat its flesh.
I eat the deer.
I eat the four bodies
over and over again.

I put a flower in your . . .

Peter Makuck

## *The Commons*

They are changing its look.
A bulldozer pierces its skin,
Noses in red depression

And mows down trees at the edge.
A derrick comes up
With jawfuls of earth, the stump

And dangling roots of an oak—
An image of Saturn
Fisting his half-eaten child.

A rust wind blows at dusk
From the diggings, dirt sifting
Back. There is nothing to help:

In our daydreams
Or the flickerings of deep sleep,
The Commons will never change:

The bell is clanging,
We gather in the sun,
The rifles are about to speak

Michael McCafferty

## *May '70*

When the steel ripped open
and the cor-ten shreds folded back
with the force of it

Something tore in his townie heart.
Barbers he'd known
guarded their bandaged poles
with shotguns
against the longhairs.

In a bank with windows boarded up
from mowers hurled through
the night before,
a teller hollers,
"They've killed four students
on the hill."

With sirens as the ambiance
another says,
"Good, that way they won't need
the ambulance."
The blast ripped wide open America.
Competition for sculpture
commemorating, diffused.

Save the commons?
Just keep that one bullet hole.
Close range, in steel.

*Seattle*
*July 1989*

63

Lowell Jaeger

## *The War At Home*

Fall of 1969. All you get for five dollars
is a membership card and a dime store medallion
chained to your wrist bearing the name
of an American POW. And a newsletter
not even your mother reads. But it delivers the war
closer to home. Also a rash under the bracelet
you refuse to remove, at the cost of itching
and tossing through sleep with ugly, foreign dreams.
Past cashing paychecks, sacking groceries
and news of an X-rated drive-in eight miles away,
your town need be no bigger than it is.
And when a handful of pot-head seniors
circle on the fifty-yard line singing
*Give Peace a Chance*, you blush and squirm
how tiny their voices, from where you stand
skeptical at your classroom window
dabbing a wet kleenex on a wrist that wants to bleed.

Maybe the same afternoon, half the Midwest between,
I'm under a sun shower, ankle deep in leprous
elm leaves, up to my ears in slogans
of savage beards and red berets. Bascom Hill
baits me with a big-city view of State Street
and the capitol dome, immaculate as a tombstone.
But I'm bored with the SDS, debating
political realities of bricks and firebombs, posturing
with our fists raised, our gas masks, our fanatic need
for public recognition and the inexplicable
loneliness that smothers me in every crowded place.
So I leave before anyone takes a vote. I opt
for the meaninglessness of French verb conjugations
and the next day I can read no significance
in the mocking editorial version of half a dozen

Weathermen who seceded from the proceedings, bothered
how their fellow anarchists were so unabashedly democratic.

Reunited with wife and babes, your POW
writes his thanks for all five dollars of your support.
Less struck by his photo than you had hoped,
your bracelet, the letter and all those dreams
become a small archive in a shoebox
under your everyday panties beside bundles
of church bulletins and notes from boys your own age.
You don't feel any more noble than six months ago
and don't expect history books listing your name.
Still, that spring your renegade seniors are stung
by the lethal facts at Kent State: four dead,
less than a hundred miles and one month away
from graduation. Meanwhile my Weathermen
have stolen wings and launched a zero-visibility
air raid on munitions plants near enough at hand
to blast me from my top bunk, completely in the dark.

After the news of Kent State I hit the streets
wanting not to miss the war at home. Block after block
I stormed the ignorant neighborhoods, wanting to yell
around each corner how the world was about to change.
I tipped some garbage cans into the gutter
and ran away. I lit a match to a stuffy
old armchair at the Salvation Army drop-box,
but it didn't want to burn. Downtown
there were barricades, but nothing beyond.
I split a smoke with a National Guardsman,
neither of us willing to share what the other wanted
to know, never coming close to the word *revolution*.
Too hard to know when and where these things take place.

Yvonne Moore Hardenbrook

## *History Lesson*

Talkin' about them killin's at Kent State
puts me in mind of Chicago's South Side in '37
when we was picketin' Republic Steel.
We marched peaceable for union rights,
not a Commie amongst us. Outa nowhere
come this solid wall of cops, charged us yellin'
RED BASTARDS, YOU GOT NO RIGHTS!
They started in shootin' and we turned tail.
Point-blank, they volleyed—them brave
back-shootin' cops. The street run red.
We carried the wounded to Sam's Bar, and
seven men cashed in on the sawdust floor.
I seen the newsreel name it a massacre
but the *Trib* never even run a line.

We had to hustle in them days. I was a
forty-two-cent nobody when I joined the union.
I didn't wear no button—a button
was a sure way to get fired. Don't see
how a boy today startin' at three-thirty-five
with ever'thing laid out for him can understand
how it was when a man was nothin' but a cipher.
It was the Big Boys called the shots.

The strike was broke, but the
Wagner Act come along and saved the union.
We never made a buck till contracts for armaments
to Europe rolled in. ARSENAL OF DEMOCRACY
the Big Boys said we was, and the war in Europe
fed our families good. SOLIDARITY FOREVER!
PROSPERITY FOR ALL!  Republic went closed shop,
the union made us strong, the Big Boys
made millions sellin' steel. The Government
chipped in . . . *they* called the shots.

66

Then it was *us* in World War II,
shippin' our sons overseas along with steel.
Prosperity, all right—ration stamps
for meat and sugar . . . shoes . . . gasoline . . .
and telegrams for GOLD STAR MOTHERS!
Thirty-three years later them kids at Kent State
was shot for marchin' peaceable,
for picketin' to protest our troops in Vietnam.
Didn't their folks never tell them
you can't win against the Big Boys?
It's WAR what sells the steel,
and the Big Boys what calls the goddam shots.

Daniel Thompson

## *May 4*

Though I come with passion to Kent
I cleave to Cleveland, oil and steel
The ghosts of John D. Rockefeller
And Margaret Bourke-White
Our river in the Flats, the Cuyahoga
A river remembering its fire, still running
Crooked as a politician past the foundry
Where the honorable statue of James A. Rhodes
Complete with briefcase, was cast
That last day before they shipped
The McVey Colossus to Columbus
A foundry worker
With a profound sense of history
Slipped the newspaper
Full of the Kent State killings
A paper he'd wrapped
Like a body bag in plastic
Into the hollow, Governor's briefcase
Now, he thought to himself
It's sealed in bronze for posterity
That gesture sub rosa
Moved the Jim Rhodes tribute
Beyond the hallowed ground of art
To the status of a time capsule
With an historical judgment
At least equal to that of the pigeons
In the fragrant, Ohio air

Bill Arthrell

## from *Kent 25*

starting that rhythm again
in my head
toes, chest.
when will i be out of here?
on a steel bed
i won't say may 4.
i'm kent 25
starting
to be proud.
i'll tell jokes to my cell mate who's in here for murder.
i'll be funny. i twist my mouth and laugh at my intent.
i'll be in the cleveland plain dealer/beacon journal/time mag.
i'm the walter mitty of the left.
dreaming
dreaming.
che gue var a.
i got a beard
he got a beard.
you can kill a revolutionary . . . .
we both got beards.
i am kinda funny
dreaming in this jail cell.
i'm very serious.
$1,000 bail
it'll kill my parents
my brother would never do this.
i got a family. uncle bob. i want him to like me.
it's dark outside
kent state quiet.
we had a revolution last spring
starting.
i threw a stick at a national guard. skinny stick.
chicken stick. not very far left stick.
they threw it back.

long fingers of bayonets.
rolling dice. cutting bullets.
stain of blood glistening prettily in the sun.
lots of sticks
very far right.
we caught them at night.
the sun blocked out many lives.
too many
perhaps 4
perhaps 25.
perhaps a whole list.
jackson state
berkeley
santa barbara
orangeburg.
i don't like this list, i muse.
i don't like this jail
cell.
the bloody stick
fingering my mind
pricking taylor hill
poking around in this gray
cell.
the rosenbergs' cell
sacco/vanzetti's cell
angela davis's cell.
i share their cell
for this night.
black in ravenna. gray november.
poet's weather.

David Shevin

## *The Discovery of Fire*

The five years of hibernation relaxed me.
I awakened just before midnight. There was blackness
in my hair and in my blood. At first I moved
very slowly, but the friction made sparks,
and stretching felt good, and then there was
a firefly, and by its light, I could see clear
across to Asia.

The calm, wavelike noises were always present.
Sometimes they sounded very loud, but I'd been
sleeping and couldn't tell. Later, a man with
a thick beard and a cloth belt told me that
the noise was the dead, returning to the place
where they'd lived. The loudness was cries
and songs and prayers. They were helping
each other. I rested on something strong.
It was near to the road, where the broad-nosed
people lived. They hunted crickets with their
fingers, stiff from reading the paper. When

I stood, I had left a mark in the remnant
of a candle, on the sculpture where the bullet
had gone through. I held a match near
the wax. I waited.

*Kent, Ohio*
*May 1975*

C. K. Williams

## *In the Heart of the Beast*

*May 1970: Cambodia, Kent State, Jackson State*

**1**

this is fresh meat right mr nixon?

this is even sweeter than mickey schwerner or fred hampton right?
even more tender than the cherokee nation or guatemala or greece
having their asses straightened for them isn't it?

this is none of your oriental imitation
this is iowa corn grown
this is jersey tomato grown
washington salmon maryland crab
this is from children
who'd barely begun ingesting corruption
the bodies floating belly up like polluted fish in cambodia
barely tainting them
the black kids blown up in their churches
hardly souring them
their torments were so meager
they still thought about life
still struggled with urgency
and compassion
so
tender

**2**

I'm sorry

I don't want to hear anymore that the innocent farmer in ohio on
   guard duty means well but is fucked up by his politicians and

72

raises his rifle out of some primal fear for his own life and his
family's and that he hates niggers hates them hates them
because he is warped and deceived by events

and pulls the trigger

I'm sorry I don't want to forgive him anymore
I don't want to say he didn't know what he was doing
because he knew what he was doing
because he didn't pull the trigger once and run away screaming
they kept shooting the kids said
we thought they were blanks but they kept shooting and shooting
we were so scared

I don't want to forgive the bricklayer from akron who might or
      might not hate his mother I don't care or the lawyer or gas
      station attendant from cleveland who may or may not have had
      a bad childhood
I don't care
I don't want to know
I don't want to hear anything about it

another kid said the rocks weren't even reaching them!

I don't want to understand why they did it

how could you?
just that

everything else is pure shit


**3**


on the front page of the times a girl is screaming
she will be screaming forever
and her friend will lie there forever you wouldn't know she wasn't
      just sleeping in the sun except for the other screaming

and on the editorial page
"the tragic nature of the division of the country . . . the provocation
    undoubtedly was great and was also unpardonable . . . "

o my god
my god

if there was a way to purify the world who would be left?
there is a list
and it says
this person for doing this
and that person for doing nothing
and this person for not howling in rage
and that for desperately hanging onto the reasons the reasons
and this list
there is an avenger
who would be left?
who is there now who isn't completely insane from all this?
who didn't dream with me last night
of burning everything destroying everyone
of tearing pieces of your own body off
of coughing your language up and spitting it away like vomit
of wanting to start at the bottom of your house
breaking everything floor by floor
burning the pictures
tearing the mattresses up
smashing windows and chairs until nothing is left
and then the cars with a sledgehammer
the markets
the stores that sell things
the buses
the bridges into the city
the airports
the international harbors
the tall buildings crumpling like corpses
the theaters torn down to the bare stage
the galleries naked the bookstores like mouths open

there should be funerals in front of the white house
bones in the capitol

Where do you stop?

how can we be like this?


**4**


I remember what it was to come downstairs
and my daughter would be there crawling toward me as fast as she
        could
crying HI DADDA HI DADDA

and what it was to bury my face in my wife's breasts and forget

to touch a friend's shoulder
to laugh
to take walks


**5**


I don't want to call anyone pig

meeting people who tell you they want war they hate communists
or somebody who'll say they hate niggers spics kikes
and you still don't believe they're beyond knowing
because you feel comfortable with them even drawn to them
and know somehow that they have salvageable hearts
you try to keep hope
for a community that could contain both of you
so that you'd both be generous and loving
and find ways that didn't need hatred and killing
to burn off the inarticulate human rage at having to die

I thought if I could take somebody like that in my arms
I could convince them that everyone was alone before death
but love saved us from living our lives reflexively with death

that it could happen
we would be naked now
we'd change now little by little
we'd be better
we would just be here
in this life

but it could be a delusion couldn't it?
it could be like thinking those soldiers were shooting blanks
up until the last second standing there scared shitless
but inside
thinking americans don't shoot innocent people!
I know it!
I learned it in school in the movies!
it doesn't happen like this
and hearing a bullet slam into the ground next to you and the flesh
and every voice in your body saying o no no
and seeing your friend go down
half her head blown away
and the image of kennedy in back of the car
and of king
and the other kennedy
and wanting to explode o no no no no no


**6**


not to be loaded up under the flopping bladewash the tubes sucking
      to be thrown out turning to flame burning on trees on grass on
      skin burning lips away breasts away genitals arms legs buttocks
not to be torn out of the pack jammed in the chamber belched out
      laid over the ground like a live fence of despair
not to fog down into the river where the fish die into the rice where
      the frogs die into the trees where the fruit dies the grain dies the
      leaves into the genes

76

into the generations

more black children
more red children
and yellow

not to be screaming

Amy Clampitt

## *The Odessa Steps*

Old lady with the pince-nez whirling,
there on the steps, to meet the bayonets—
would she, given, in that twinkling of an
eyeglass smashed, the option, have gone home
and shut the door before the trouble started,
preferring ikon and samovar to all those changes,
promises of an upheaval far too heady
to be kept: or would she have declared
that to have died there, where the action was,
inhaling an ozone that only in transit
tastes like splendor, was to have been lucky?

Dark mother of an ailing boy, aghast
as at a long atrocity exhumed, the damp
of catacombs still on it: shade
from the same cleft that opened, halfway
around the world, on an Ohio hillside
where shots were fired—a kneeling,
incredulous dark girl's mouthed O
the Soviet cinema's unconscious ape:
a runaway, picked up two years after
for loitering with intent, her moment of
pure grief, fame's discard, an unhoused ruin.

Wheels of the upended baby carriage
flailing, there on the steps, a visionary
metaphor derailed: where are the wheels
Ezekiel saw ablaze, where are the eyes,
the voice, the noise of many waters?
Who looked for openings, for signs
of a new age beginning, finds instead
a shutdown: these gray lives' torpor,

the labor gangs, the litter on the freeway,
fleered-at shapes of windmills gone rotten,
the Satanic millwheels still grinding.

Alicia Ostriker

## *Cambodia*

My son Gabriel was born on May 14, 1970, during the Vietnam War, a few days after the United States invaded Cambodia, and a few days after four students had been shot by National Guardsmen at Kent State University in Ohio during a protest demonstration.

On May 1, President Nixon announced Operation Total Victory, sending 5,000 American troops into Cambodia to destroy North Vietnamese military sanctuaries, in a test of "our will and character," so that America would not seem "a pitiful helpless giant" or "accept the first defeat in its proud 190-year history."
He wanted his own war.

> The boy students stand in line
> at Ohio State
> each faces a Guardsman in gasmask
> each a bayonet point at his throat.

US air cavalry thrusts into Kompong Cham province, seeking bunkers. Helicopters descend on "The Parrot's Beak." B-52s heavily bomb Red sanctuaries. Body count! Body count high! in the hundreds. The President has explained, and explains again, that this is not an invasion.

Monday, May 4th, at Kent State, laughing demonstrators and rock-throwers on a lawn spotted with dandelions. It was after a weekend of beerdrinking. Outnumbered Guardsmen, partially encircled and out of tear gas, begin to retreat uphill, turn, kneel, in unison aim their guns. Four students lie dead, seventeen wounded. 441 colleges and universities strike, many shut down.
The President says: "When dissent turns to violence, it invites tragedy."

A veteran of the Khe Sanh says: "I saw enough violence, blood and death and I vowed never again, never again . . . Now I must protest.

I'm not a leftist but I can't go any further. I'll do damn near anything to stop the war now."

A man in workclothes tries to seize an American flag from a student. "That's my flag! I fought for it! You have no right to it! . . . To hell with your movement. We're fed up with your movement. You're forcing us into it. We'll have to kill you." An ad salesman in Chicago: "I'm getting to feel like I'd actually enjoy going out and shooting some of these people, I'm just so goddamned mad."

One, two, three, four, we don't want! your fucking war!

They gathered around the monument, on the wet grass, Dionysiac, beaded, flinging their clothes away. New England, Midwest, Southwest, cupfuls of innocents leave the city and buy farmland. At the end of the frontier, their backs to the briny Pacific, buses of tourists gape at the acid-dropping children in the San Francisco streets. A firebomb flares. An electric guitar bleeds.

Camus: "I would like to be able to love my country and still love justice."

Some years earlier, my two daughters were born, one in Wisconsin at a progressive university hospital where doctors and staff behaved affectionately, one in England where the midwife was a practical woman who held onto my feet and when she became impatient with me said: PUSH, Mother. Therefore I thought I knew what childbirth was supposed to be: a woman *gives birth* to a *child*, and the medical folk assist her.

But in the winter of 1970 I had arrived five months pregnant in Southern California, had difficulty finding an obstetrician who would take me, and so was now tasting normal American medical care. It tasted like money. During my initial visit to his ranch-style offices on a street where the palm trees lifted their heads into the smog like a row of fine mulatto ladies, Dr. Keensmile called me "Alicia" repeatedly, brightly, benignly, as if I were a child or a servant. I hated him right away. I hated his suntan. I knew he was untrue to his wife. I was sure he played golf. The routine delivery anesthetic for him and his group was a spinal block, he said. I explained that I would not need a spinal since

81

I had got by before on a couple of cervical shots, assumed that deliveries were progressively easier, and wanted to decide about drugs myself when the time came. He smiled tolerantly at the ceiling. I remarked that I liked childbirth. I remarked that childbirth gave a woman an opportunity for supreme pleasure and heroism. He smiled again. They teach them, in medical school, that pregnancy and birth are diseases. He twinkled. Besides, it was evident that he hated women. Perhaps that was why he became an obstetrician. Just be sure and watch your weight, Alicia. Smile.

I toyed, as I swelled and bulged like a watermelon, with the thought of driving out into the Mohave to have the baby. I continued my visits to Dr. Keensmile. I did not talk to Dr. Keensmile about Cambodia. I did not talk to him about Kent State. *Sauve qui peut.* You want a child of life, stay away from psychic poison. In the waiting room I found pamphlets which said that a newborn baby must be fed on a strict schedule, as it needed the discipline, and that one must not be moved by the fact that it would cry at first, as this was good for it, to start it out on the right foot. And my daughters were laughing at me for my difficulty in buckling their sandals.

In labor, I discovered that I could have an enjoyable time if I squatted on the bed, rocked a little while doing my breathing exercises, and sang songs in my head. The bed had muslin curtains drawn around it; nobody would be embarrassed by me. So I had settled into a melody and had been travelling downstream with it for some long duration, when a nurse came through the curtains, stork white, to ask if I was ready for my shot. Since the pains were becoming strong and I felt unsure about keeping control through the transitional stage of labor, which is the hardest, I said fine, expecting a local. This would temporarily alleviate the pain of the fast-stretching cervix, leaving other muscles free.

Of course, it was a sedative. I grew furry. They lay me down. I was eight fingers dilated, only five or seven minutes away from the final stage of labor, where a woman needs no drugs because she becomes a goddess. Then Dr. Keensmile appeared to ask if I was ready for my spinal. A faint flare of "no" passed, like a moonbeam. Because of the Demerol, if they had asked me whether I was ready to have my head severed, I probably would have said yes. Drool ran from my mouth. Yes, I said.

When they wheeled me to the delivery room, I fought to maintain wakeful consciousness despite the Demerol, and fought to push, with my own body, to give birth to my child myself, despite the fact that I could feel nothing—nothing at all—below the waist, as if I did not exist there, as if I had been cut in half and bandaged.

A stainless place. I am conscious, only my joy is cut off. I feel the stainless will of everyone. Nothing red in the room. I am sweating. Death.

The black-haired head, followed by the supple limbs, emerges in the mirror. The doctor says it is a boy. Three thoughts fall, like file cards. One: Hooray! We made it! Finito! Two: YOU SONOFABITCHING BASTARD, NEXT TIME I'M GOING TO DO THIS RIGHT. Three: What next time?

Our bodies and our minds shoot into joy, like trees into leaves. Playfulness as children, sex, work with muscles, work with brains. Some bits survive, where we are lucky, or clever, or we fight. The world will amputate what it can, wanting us cripples. Cut off from joy, how many women conceive? Cut off, how many bear? And cut, how many give birth to their children? Now I am one of them. I did not fight. Beginning a day after my son's birth, and continuing for a week, I have swordlike headaches, which I attribute to the spinal. I am thirty-three. In the fall I will be back at work, back East. My husband and I have two daughters, both all right so far, and now the son for whom we were hoping. There will never be a next time.

What does this have to do with Cambodia?

Denise Levertov

## *The Day the Audience Walked Out on Me, and Why*

*(May 8th, 1970, Goucher College, Maryland)*

Like this it happened:
after the antiphonal reading from the psalms
and the dance of lamentation before the altar,
and the two poems, *Life at War* and *What Were They Like*,
I began my rap,
and said:

Yes, it is well that we have gathered
in this chapel to remember
the students shot at Kent State,

but let us be sure we know
our gathering is a mockery unless
we remember also
the black students shot at Orangeburg two years ago,
and Fred Hampton murdered in his bed
by the police only months ago.

And while I spoke the people
—girls, older women, a few men—
began to rise and turn
their backs to the altar and leave.

And I went on and said,
Yes, it is well that we remember
all of these, but let us be sure
we know it is hypocrisy
to think of them unless
we make our actions their memorial,
actions of militant resistance.

By then the pews were almost empty
and I returned to my seat and a man stood up
in the back of the quiet chapel
(near the wide-open doors through which
the green of May showed, and the long shadows
                                of late afternoon)
and said my words
desecrated a holy place.

And a few days later
when some more students (black) were shot
at Jackson, Mississippi,
no one desecrated the white folks' chapel,
because no memorial service was held.

Lucille Clifton

## *after Kent State*

only to keep
his little fear
he kills his cities
and his trees
even his children    oh
people
white ways are
the way of death
come into the
Black
and live

Maxine Scates

## *The Teacher*

*to the memory of Ann Stanford*

On the day I learned of your death
my friends asked me to read to them.
It was raining,
midsummer in a farmhouse.
I read one poem
the poem that begins with a line from one of yours
*It has been falling for weeks now*
and I didn't tell them. I couldn't tell them
what I'd known all day.


This was the first year
I could have told you what it was like at twenty,
could have seen, do see
how every morning
I sat on the stone bench
by the mock orange trees
waiting for you to walk by on your way to class.
I'm on that bench waiting.
I've been waiting for years.
I'm at the arena ushering roller derby.
I'm selling tickets at the Queen Mary.
I'm shoulder-to-shoulder in the hallways after Cambodia.
I'm watching the helicopters overhead
because Reagan has shut down
every state college in California.


I understand nothing.
I've barely made it this far.
But every morning I sit on the stone bench
because it is all I have
because I'm in love
waiting for you, a woman, a poet, to pass:

I've found you and I've read all your books.
I've read the poems until they are in me.
I take the lines
and scatter them around the woman
who stands in front of the class
because I want to see how each word falls into a life.
And that begins it,
that begins the life of the word.
If I read now what I wrote then
I can remember every word you said.
I can remember sitting there head down
saying nothing,
until finally I read a poem out to the class
and you said: "There, there
you've done it."

Later that evening
when I did tell my friends, they asked
"What was it?"
"How did she touch you?"
And I answered that after awhile
you said: "I can't teach you anymore *now*."
And when you said *now*
I knew you believed I could learn more.

I didn't tell them about the first night
I came to your house,
winding my way up the canyon
arriving early before the others.
I sat outside in my car
watching you move in the kitchen,
a woman ordinary enough there in that circle of light.
I was afraid.
I wanted so much. I didn't know
what you could see in me
but I wanted to see it in you. Years later
you told me you knew I was out there.
And later that night,
for the first time up all night writing,

I began to know there was something outside my life
that my life would go on day by day
but there would be something else.
It was there
in the wind, in the walnuts, in that canyon.
I remembered the white horse.
I remembered the line
*Where is the white horse?*
I remembered the towhees drowning in the trough
as if I were there on that hillside with you
in the wind—that wind—
so then I knew eucalyptus,
I knew it swinging over the road on the way
to the state hospital to visit my grandmother
on Sundays, the cars pulled to the side,
the passengers stealing tomatoes from the fields.
I'd had no memory,
I didn't know where I came from
and now you were listening
and though all I could see then was loss
now I knew there was a story.

But I did tell them that it was years
before I understood
that I was beginning to learn the rest of what
I had to learn,
before I understood that what you had seen in me
didn't belong to me at all.
That was your gift to me—
there—that was the place
where my life bent away from itself
to join something else,
just as when we say
it did not happen to only me
we begin to give up the self,
saying it happens to all of us
and that is when we begin to hear
and to speak and to give up our silence.

Earlier that evening
when I had said nothing
I looked out at the rain
thinking of another time
when after a long journey
I had come home changed
to a pouring rain in midsummer—
as I stood on the porch
one of the Bach cello suites,
that exquisite music
the bow of the cellist
laboring, occasionally scraping the strings,
played behind the curtain of rain
until music and rain flowed together—
and then, on that evening,
I thought, I am remembering you,
*I will remember you into light*
the dense rain,
the others moving in the kitchen behind me,
and the green field on an evening in July
where through the window I saw the chair
the child had dragged out earlier in the day
to sit and read under the only tree,
a huge oak that drew the field around it.

Ann Stanford

## *Our Town*

This is the village where we grew
Our fathers and their sires in line
The trees they planted shade the view
And the white houses shine.

The families here had come to stay
The preacher was the parson's son
And if one brother moved away
We kept the solid one.

We tended order in the town
Our lawns were trim, our hedges green
And in the countryside around
The furrows straight and clean.

We went to church, obeyed the laws
And voted on election day.
The peaceful farms surrounded us
The battles always far away.

And when the soldiers came to town
With drums and our flag overhead,
We watched them from the commons lawn
Until they shot us dead.

*IV*

Louise McNeill

## *The Three Suns*

(Twentieth Century)

"Three suns come up before a war,"
The old folks used to tell—
"Three suns come rising up the sky
In crimson parallel—"

So in our time twelve suns arose
To count the sons who fell.

Ernest Bryll

## *Prayer for the Time of Advent*

God save us from hatred
Leave a bitter seed of remembrance
So that in us the close ones live
Those who were taken in the advent

God give us the dark pride of silence
But leave us the power to disdain
Those who laugh at humiliation
So that for them Poland may turn into a stone

God calm evil and rancor in us
Help those who are sinful in stupidity
Keep mercy from them—a sacred leaf
When they are half-departed from the nation

God change into brightness a candle
Which we set out in our windows
For we have only as much of our country
As there is truth and blood left in us

God help us when it is stone-heavy
To look at this candle tremble and die
Before it heaves itself as the Bethlehem Star
So that each face may be seen

God do not let us lose ourselves
Before disrupted darkness comes crushing
So that we might look into our friends' faces
And the friends might look at us

*translated by Dorota Sobieska*

Daniel Bourne

## *The Language of the Dead*

One of those days when the earth
seems to make its own light, even during a hard rain
the autumn leaves radiant. We have just visited
the grave of a murdered Polish priest. We watched
workmen cut flowers and put them in vases. Later,
we buy postcards in the church kiosk: the battered body
fished out of the reservoir; the village road sign
where he was kidnapped; each photo a station
of the twentieth century cross. Such a day

weights the earth. When we go home to warm tea,
to the heat of our bodies, the heft of our dictionaries
with their broken spines, we try to break through
to the language of the dead. Tomorrow,
we will shop in the stores, but no one
will acknowledge our presence.

*Warsaw*
*October 1985*

97

Joseph Bruchac

## *Crossing into West Germany*

There are borders on earth
and lines on the maps,
colors and barriers, human names
stuck onto the soil, as if earth could claim
to understand or speak our tongues,
as if the hawks looking down in long flight
saw nations and flags, not forests and valleys,
place to live, to hunt, care for their young.

But the wind still blows
over every border
and the soil that sifts
through the hands of farmers
responds the same
to drought and rain.

Ask me now
to which nation
I belong
and I will answer
without words in a song,
that language all
our ancestors spoke,
learned from the flow
of clear streams to the sea,
birds chanting praise
to each dawn.

Karen Kovacik

## *Käthe Kollwitz,*
## *After a Visit to the New Russia, 1927*

My model sleeps. But no matter—
the body slumped is a poem too.
Calloused hands open into petals.
The smudge between her lips
softens to an oval. Her neck
the color of bread and potatoes.

As a girl I probed for the ribs
under the skin of cats. Could I
have become a surgeon? Instead,
I put paper between me
and the body. Bones appeared.
Flesh. The freckled arm of a woman.
Her fingers closing the eyes
on her husband's swollen face.

How could I not observe?

Now I am old. I bend over this work
like a heavy bird. I breathe
with my eyes, praying for the star
to rise out of nowhere. In Moscow
I watched the rags on women's feet.
Even there hunger rattles on
like an empty train.

# Osip Mandelstam

## *394*

Toward the empty earth
falling, one step faltering—
some sweetness, in this
unwilling hesitance—

she walks, keeping
just ahead of her friends,
the quick-footed woman,
the young man, one year younger.

A shy freedom draws her, her hobbled step
frees her, fires her, and it seems
the shining riddle in her walk
wants to hold her back:

the riddle, that this spring weather
is for us the first mother:
the mother of the grave.
And this will keep on beginning forever.


There are women,
the damp earth's flesh and blood:
every step they take, a cry,
a deep steel drum.

It is their calling
to accompany those who have died;
and to be there, the first
to greet the resurrected.

To ask for their tenderness
would be a trespass against them;

but to go off, away from them—
no one has the strength.

Today an angel; tomorrow
worms, and the grave;
and the day after
only lines in chalk.

The step you took
no longer there to take.

Flowers are deathless. Heaven is round.
And everything to be is only a promise.

Voronezh<br>May 4, 1937

translated by Jean Valentine<br>and Anne Frydman

Angela Bilia

## *Red Carnations*

*for the students killed in Athens, Greece*
*November 17, 1973*

They had occupied what belonged to them
and camped out in the streets.
They were the crowds of silenced voices,
young and old together for the first time
under the fall sky, under the flags
of white communion with red letters
like coyotes howling in the dark
the song of bread, education, and freedom.
ΨΩΜΙ ΠΑΙΔΕΙΑ ΕΛΕΥΘΕΡΙΑ

Then there was light, and chaos followed order,
when the ruler's sword fell, when the word cut.
The hands held out the weapons of love,
flowers and songs and youthful blood.
The arms held on to the iron gate, the line
between those who die and those who live.
The eyes of those buried under were torches
that led the silent dirge of victory.

The city was awake, the country listened.
The voice came clear, unmistakable.
Each word, a knife blade flew
suicidal in the thin night air.
Another wounded winter lay angry and bitter.
*3:15 a.m., Athens: the school of the Polytechnic*
*is now free, the gate is down, order is restored.*

The order the war generation resisted
in underground Morse-code heart beats;
the order my brothers' fingertips felt
on the cold asphalt at 3:15 in the morning;

the order my eleven-year-old eyes watched
on a black and white screen
the black and white truth
of a tank crushing red carnations.

Michael Waters

## *The Torches*

*Nicaragua*

Limbs lopped off, the fathers
thrashed through the orchard
till a torch was touched to their hair
and they were consumed by the unearthly
love that lifted their souls toward heaven.
How impossible to mute the body with belief.
Women closed their shutters and crossed themselves.
Soldiers jeered. But the burning were beyond
the grievous clamor of the New World.

Clear sky that night, the thousand stars
assuming tentative shapes
like children assembling in the schoolyard.
The ashes smoldered on the hillside.
Then rain. By morning, only chipped dice and the scorched
    soil remained.

What's irrefutable is that sweeping odor,
not the fume of charred tongues and gasoline,
but the first profuse blossoming of orchids,
a fragrant exhalation from the earth's core,
and those sudden shafts of light
crisscrossing in the late afternoon
as the missing bear through the marketplace
their flaming tapers of spine, their wicks of hair.

James Ragan

## *Lombardo at Midnight, New Year's Eve, 1972*

*for the Vietnam MIAs*

It was neither the fire we trimmed
like hair, thick and full
of body, nor the wood

we cut for fuel out of spruce—
that warmed us, took us back
to you, back to our roots. Their use

came later during crow
fights on the ledge where we planted
bread and watched the new

year falling like a beak
on pale snow. We wanted memories
of the moon hitting ground,

a crowd to count it down,
to seconds, to the moment
of impact, some new force

pulling on our blood, a rose
growing out of flesh,
out of season with its seed. We needed

rhythm, a new song for the birth
of Eve. We wanted that and more,
a story for the song we called *ennui*.

Instead you gave us back
the bricks and mortar, our beds to lie in,
forefathers in sleep, tracking down the alien

creed—Live and let die, for peace sake—
our heroes, name tags on their genitals.
You gave us back their schedule,

crucifixion by time-clock, your woodwinds
blowing the same red ball off its edge
like a man falling head-first into earth.

Christopher Howell

# *Liberty & Ten Years of Return*

*for the veterans*

## I

In the singed breath of London
we were lost
and aching sailors burnt by ships.
Disgusted, lonely, broke we four
buddies went adrift, sealed
casks of withered lust. Above the dim
lamps our President kept saying, "No.
We love a rigid chaos. Get laid
if you like, but nobody leaves."

## II

A few cops passed like blue
trees moving. A taxi splashed dark
on our dark American frowns.
Hours we spoke of the trains, chanting,
mythical; of penalties
for missing muster, ship's movement,
the long glide home. At last, shivering
we stared down years of open windows
till the third-class cars pulled out
for Portsmouth in the teeth of dawn.

## III

None of us expected this
arrival, the band strewn dead
on an empty pier, the fleet crusted

and opening like a bowl of dazed peonies
to the chalk sky. Now
we see:  ours is an absent life, no healing.
Sent over the great sea
a decade has returned us with no riches,
no message, and no home waiting
or wanting us here.

Kevin Stein

## *Portraits*

It's not the chapel bell at Arles,
only a doorbell rung on television,
but it's enough to send the dog
in a scurry and yapping to the front door
where no one is. I'm not Gauguin,
at least not now, the isle of Tahiti
has disappeared into the ether of possibility,
and the girls, too. All a dream.
What's there to say but *yes*,
these are my legs and doughy middle,
this is my face beginning to wrinkle,
these hands mine, blunt-fingered, small.
Yes, it's only the house I've been painting
on long summer days, and no, nothing's exotic
about my dreaming of the islands,
a place I longed for but never got to
in my unbridled youth. Maybe it's
the heat, or maybe the paint,
but I imagined us sitting in the almost
fluorescent ocean, under a great inverted bowl
of blue sky, drinking beer in the afternoon.
*This*, for chrissake, this could've happened
as easily as it didn't for me and my friend Dana,
who, wounded at Da Nang, came home
to kiss my sister on our front porch
as if it were nothing. He gave her
a black velvet Elvis. A forlorn,
sort of disembodied Elvis
whose brown eyes looked as evanescent
as the voice of reason in 1969.
Then he went back, and didn't
come back. This morning's heat so rose
like a blister from the shingles, and waves
so shimmered above a green sea of beans

that the beauty of dog in shade,
child in red wagon, and wife in garden
offered an angle of declamation I'd seen
once in Gauguin's "Riders on the Beach."
Four riders depart under a turbulent sky,
while pale riders on still paler horses
intersect their path unseen. Gauguin
thought of the pale ones as spirits, as life
playing out its endless what might've beens,
as even now I stand at the burst-open screen door
and call, *Come home boy, come home*,
unable to see or hear what's out there,
what's not.

Jim Daniels

## *A Real Comedian:  The True Genius of Bob Hope*

Was he ever really funny? When? I want to know.
Are clowns ever really funny, even to children?
Do you really have to go to college to be a clown?

Why is the President a clown? What training has he had?
Do you really have to go to Hamburger U.?

I had a girlfriend who went on tour with a mime troupe.
For months afterward, she kept making that big O

of surprise. She thought it was cute when I got mad.
O. Let's all be mimes. Or do we have to go

to the Marcel Marceau school of mimery? The President
is a mime. Look how he holds his hand to his ear

look how he shrugs. Can you guess? He is being
an idiot. Here's the scary part:

that Bob Hope's friend can be President.
That the President can laugh at Bob Hope

like the French laugh at Jerry Lewis.
At least Dean stopped pretending he liked Jerry

at least Bing sang "Drummer Boy" with David Bowie.
Is there a college for becoming Bob Hope?

Is his vault full of jokes there, a whole vault
without one chuckle? Bob entertained the troops

yes, he gets a little goodwill for that.
They laughed at his jokes, but they were desperate.

How many of them would have showed up
if he didn't have his bimbos along? Bob

always has bimbos. Brooke is his latest.
Look how she shakes her head when she smiles.
It's called acting. She learned that from Calvin.

The President married a ghost and hosted
Death Valley Days. 20 Mule Team Borax—
What does that mean? I have never understood

the true genius of his acting ability.
I have never understood why America voted for him

twice. Who's pulling his strings? His head
shakes like Brooke's. Suspiciously like Brooke's.

All the bimbos on his specials know how to make the O.
Bob tells a joke, they make the O.

O Bob you are old and I should not make fun of you
but you are still on tv. What's so special
about your specials? Maybe you were good in the 40s

or 50s, or even the early 60s. Maybe you were funny
then, before Vietnam. Packy East. I like that name.

A real name. A lousy boxer. A bad mime. The whole country's
falling apart, and we're stuck with you and George Burns.

We're stuck with you and George Bush. We're stuck
with Bush and Dan Quayle. Dan and Brooke.

Bob, you won't go away. You won't take your millions
and millions and leave us alone. You are so rich

it makes me so sad. You have to be rich
to be the President's friend, the President for 8 years

count 'em. 1. 2. 3. 4. 5. 6. 7. 8. has made me so sad
I am losing my words, I am losing

my O of surprise. All I can do
is the scene where the walls are closing in.

*December 1988*

Frank Polite

## *Considering the Source*

Out one day to dig up a few potatoes
in the field, your spade hits on
something solid. It has the familiar
ring of marble, which in your
part of the world is no big thing.

You dig in sideways to get around it,
and around it, and you dig, until
you uncover what appears to be
a seashell, or human ear, or nostril.
You call the local archaeologist

and in no time at all, you got
the biggest potato imaginable: a two
ton head of milky marble that
snarls out at you the meanest baby
face you ever saw. Of course,

being a peasant, you don't recall
Edward G. Robinson portraying a car-
toon version of that face in
*Little Caesar;* still, you know well
enough that cruelty is not bio-

degradable; some things never change.
In this case, Caesar turns out to
be Domitian, a law and order
paranoid who killed off nearly half
of Rome, before his wife, his

friends, and a steward named Steph-
anus knifed him in the groin.
That night you dream of a huge marble

man swimming under your field.
You run like hell, not knowing where

on Earth this monstrous being
will surface—a scene, by the way,
right out of the movie, *Jaws*,
but you don't know about that either.
Awake, you are history now,

forgotten, and that enormous head
of Domitian is in Izmir's Antiquities
Museum, a minor tourist attraction.
Suetonius tells us a lot
about Domitian, but for my own

bad dream, one detail is sufficient:
*Throughout every gladiatorial*
*show, Domitian would chat, sometimes*
*in very serious tones, with*
*a little boy who had a grotesquely*

*small head, and always stood*
*at his knee dressed in red. Once he*
*was heard to ask the child,*
*"Can you guess why I just appointed*
*Mettius Rufus Prefect of Egypt?"*

Suetonius doesn't tell us
what the boy guessed, or why Domitian
appointed Mettius Rufus
Prefect of Egypt. We are left
to consider the source:

a peasant, a few potatoes,
a couple of grotesque heads unearthed;
and all of History, it seems,
all the long and cruel cinema of being,
to answer an insane question.

# Jonathan Williams

the fbi files on
the late emile de
antonio included the information
that when he was
10 years old he
told someone he wanted
to be an eggplant
when he grew up

Edward Field

## *The Scream*

AIDS IS GERM WARFARE AGAINST HOMOSEXUALS
screams the poster, pasted up around the city,
probably hand-printed in a cellar by some certifiable crazy
making connections, out of a terrible clarity of mind,
like revolving red flashes of alarm—

CIA . . . PENTAGON . . . FUNDAMENTALISTS . . . SECRET
LABS . . . BIOLOGICAL ENGINEERING . . . EQUATORIAL
AFRICA . . . HUMAN GUINEA PIGS . . . EXPENDABLE POPULATIONS . . .

*and all it took was a few*
*doctored poppers sold at bathhouses*
*in New York and San Francisco,*
*and in one blow, sexual freedom, gay*
*liberation, gone*

Yes, and as a bonus, drug addicts.

It's crackpot, of course, hard to believe
anyone is that loony to manufacture this virus,
much less release it on earth. More likely,
it's only nature's latest attempt
to reduce the population, in which case
it doesn't matter who gets it in the neck
or how it spreads.

Either way, the poster's scream
of pain and paranoia is in its essence
true—there's been a war
between man and microbe from the beginning.
And if AIDS is secretly a plot against homosexuals,
it is also, and becoming more so every day,
GERM WARFARE AGAINST HUMANITY.

117

Ed Ochester

## *Oh, By the Way*

My friend April Fallon tells me
that blood on the exterior of the brain
is cooler than that in the interior
and that it's in the cooler blood
that dreams reside.
What do you think?
Do you love the head as much as I do?
That calcareous shell, the stoniest part
of the body. And the stone
within the skull, the maker of imperatives,
of absolutes, that directed the trains
to the death camps. The brain
has no nerves to feel pain,
that stone that gave assent
to the show trials—that Stalinist part
of the body—and the saturation bombings,
Cambodia, Dresden, you name them.
What do you think?
The overexamined life isn't worth living.
That veil of cool blood
where dreams reside: there even now
an old scholar rests his eyes
behind his hands; the farmer exerts
the requisite pressure on the cow's teats
for milk, in that pastoral memory;
the old woman wracked by pertussis
will be saved from her poverty.
Thin cool veil of blood.
What do you think?
I have to stop writing about love.
I have to stop making sense.
Cool veil of blood, old dreams:

Jeffords pushed against the bronze
school doors, red stain on white shirt,
kid with the knife:
"motherfuckin motherfucker"
(deconstruct that);
the child whispering, "Help me help me."
O thin veil of blood
where dreams reside
cool veil of blood

William Studebaker

## *Trace Elements Around the Saylor Creek Bombing Range*

We accept the dilapidated cabin
as the end of the road,
park the truck, front wheels
turned toward the hillside,
wedging rocks tightly under tires,
an extra hitch
so she won't roll off while we're gone.

Beyond the cabin, the rock corral,
the fence that keeps to the ground,
as if the landscape might wander away,
a trail sputters in and out
of a dry creek bed,
then staggers through a grove
of Rocky Mountain Juniper

(the smell of gin . . . faint
among the flakes of parched snow).

As we duck under the trees
(limbs neck-high), a kingbird shrieks,
and coyotes abandon their tracks
where the trail veers up
past small caves and rock shelters,
where no one's been home
for five hundred years.

(What if we lived here? Turned the truck
loose from her tether at the end of the road?)

What if we lived here, and this storm,
broken once by a bird's screech
and again by its wings,
as flight feathers scuffed the cold air,
settled in and, settling in,
became all we know of next door
and all we want of grace?

The river . . . not far,
a trip we'd take every day,
and today we take it and stand on ripples
that leaped and never came down:
something of how time was,
of how the world is the same:
earth, fire, wind, and water.

*Winter Solstice 1990*

*V*

James Broughton

## *For a Gathering of Poets*

Poets of the world, ignite!
Brighten your beacon words.
Blaze into flames of speech.
Listeners in bewildered dark
hunger for sounds of light.

Sing out tonics for the wounded heart.
Lend a throat to the tongue-tied soul.
Lullaby the shuddering flesh of the damned.
Pierce deaf ears with hallelujah hopes.
Exult in rallying roars of renewal.

Poets are not gnats in the wind.
They are dragonflies from the sun.
Come, burn your bliss in midair.
You are more needed than you know.
Be arsonists of the phoenix nest
and glow!

Lawson Fusao Inada

## *From Ancient to Present:*
## *Homage to Kent State*

An old pond.
A frog jumps in—
The sound of water!

Twenty years later.
Many frogs emerge—
The sound of water!

David Hassler

## *May 1990*

the ground is beginning again
to forgive the long winter

and responds to the bottoms of my feet
treading across the field

the brown tufts and stubble grass
crack like stiff sponge

and soon will give way to green
there are times I can cling to a branch

feel its bending
in the curve of my hand

and fall back spreading my arms
to the lightness of the sun

I've learned how to shout at the buds
breaking through their winter shields

tightly wrapped leaf upon leaf
they remain in their pursed lips

until they unfold
as a slow whisper

sometimes I wonder about
the chambers of my heart

if like small Chinese boxes
they treasure only air

inside these quiet parlors
I remain a connoisseur of seasons

and patiently do the work
I hope will turn green

Brenda Hillman

## *White Deer*

*for May 4th, Kent State*

I was angry at the absent father of the world
so I followed the little stream.
Deep in the woods it went with its rusty needs,

and there in the divided meadow
one white deer fed in the drought-starved rushes.

Others fed beside it
but no other white ones, only
six brown mule-tailed ones who scarcely looked up.
And I had the company of anger
which rose and fell.
I'd been trying to compose some words to the hurt earth,
seeing the layer of haze in the hills,
was thinking all the poems had been taken back,
all the poems were being used up far from here.

Something priestly about that grazing buck.
He seemed self-conscious in his central whiteness.
I'd only heard rumors of his presence in the park.
Perhaps the luck of the earth is changing—
some parallel life
brought back from its secret chambers.

I could use that deer as a symbol—for what?
Tried to forgive its careless elegance,
looked closely at the tender, fur-edged antlers
pushing out
and loved their soft risings—
poor thing, just a baby really—

but what did it stand for?
I've taught too much literature . . .

In dreams things often enter
from the left, then move right
like reading; that's how the deer vanished,
looking up once,
and I had my anger, its helpless purity. Where
did it come from, why, what
can I use it for?

Mort Krahling

## *Spring: Kent*

**1**

It comes, as ever, far after
the time we had chosen.
And even come, some slight chill
remains. To be found unexpected
like a box full of old mail.

**2**

Voices hang in the trees
along the river, under the bridge
and I must listen
carve out meaning, throw bread
to small white ducks, suck at
rotting teeth, come home
with a twelve pack of beer, a can
of Campbell's potato soup. The white cat
comes out from the trailer hitch.
I feed, he feeds. There is no mail.
In thirteen days
I will be thirty-one. And it's on.
The whole thing is on.
The end of the year suicides hang
in cascades of light. And it's on.
On with the water, the voices in the water
on with the sunlight shining
beneath the water. I imagine coils
of thick wet hair, anchored
against the current.

Jean-Claude van Itallie

## *Letter to a Friend*

Of course I remember when it happened—
It's like remembering where you were when Kennedy was killed,
Or King.
When the Kent killings happened,
I called you—do you remember?—
To ask if you were okay.
Silly. Why shouldn't you be okay?
But you are my friend in Kent,
And calling you connected me,
Made truer my feeling
That it happened to friends.

What did you say to me?
I don't remember.
What was there to say?
What is there to say now?

The time for indignation has surely passed.
But there remains that sickening awe,
The realization that unthinkable Ignorance lives in us
And can result in unthinkable deaths.

What was it Ronny Laing wrote twenty-five years ago?
Something about the unacknowledged parts of ourselves
Walking the earth like automatons committing murder?

What can I do about it?

Isn't that the question?
Question:
What unacknowledged part of me
Still strides mindlessly off to war
While I remain peacefully at home
Believing I am fully self-controlled?

What can we do?

Only mark that it happened.
And in marking, "it happened,"
To feel fully all the deep hurts
That mark each our own heart.

And in marking "it happened,"
I also vow
Not to rest smug
In any single concept,
Not to be self-righteous.

And I rejoice
In our friendship,
Which has lasted twenty years beyond the catastrophe.
I rejoice in the touching here of
Open-hearted people
Come together to mourn
And so to commune.

*Boulder, Colorado*
*April 19, 1990*

# Alex Gildzen

*if you want to write you just sit your*
*ass down in a chair and begin to type*
                              *—Ed Ochester*

the gathering approaches
& I choke

                              no poems

since november

& everyday a friend
sends new poems
to be read
when the poets
converge on Kent

Maggie says
it's for remembrance
& healing
this gathering
this reading of poems

I remember
when words
peltd the page
like bullets
when we tried
to stop a war

for my generation
there was Vietnam
& there is AIDS

I remember
the brave soldiers

134

who died
in both undeclard wars

maybe these months
of silence
mean I can't stop AIDS
with words
anymore than
my generation
stoppd that war
with poems

but we need to try
to pit craft against chaos
to say the words
to spirit the spirit
to set the agenda
for healing

the gathering approaches
& I sit my ass down
writing these words
wondering
if they're a poem
wondering
if I'll read this
wondering
how many friends
will send more poems
wondering
how many friends
will live another day

*April 19, 1990*

Michael Dennis Browne

## *May Four*

*for the students of Kent State*

Green, if you can bear to be
on earth again, as if earth
wept up her longing in green,
rooms of longing broken open by rain,
if trees can agree to being
robed again in blossom, as though
all blood that has flooded the ground
these twenty years returns
twined with the rain into shapes
such as the seas only over
centuries of grinding can fashion,

how then will *we* not say
that these we meet to honor
have soaked our own speech and song,
say they live again,
cells of our syllables, climbing,
as second by second the breath
renews in us, the survivors?
Whoever remains, us, whoever
is spared, us, how not to say
we give out our lives
not in the name of our single selves
but twined with the silent ones,
as unbelievably we breathe
those breaths denied our sisters
and brothers of breath.

Whatever it is that wants
everything down, everything done with,
stripped, spoiled, the earth over,
the rivers rotten, the fields

136

scraped of their seed, the pitiable
cities silent, their throats
wrapped round by their own
corroded streets, whatever it is
that wants these deaths forgotten,
plowed under, whoever, whatever
infiltrates the rain, stamps
*cancelled* on the seas, whispers
into the ears of the trees lies, lies,
who shreds the secrets of ancestors,
entombs the very smoke of their fires,

let that not be ever the only voice,
let that not go unanswered,
unnamed, ever, not be our signal
sent either to distant stars
and worlds which may or may not
be living, or into those lives
that look to ours, the children,
those worlds expecting that seeds
of the believing, not the despairing life,
be sown in them.

Allison, Jeffrey, Sandra, William,
what to say to *them*, the children,
in your name, in our voices
your imagined voices feed?
Say, perhaps or at least, this:
that the earth is not over,
as late in the terrible century
the war is not over, that we
continue to breathe on the spark,
again, again, for them as for ourselves,
all the while imagining flame,

say to these daughters and sons
whom you were denied, that into
the warring world where green
and rain and May can bear to be

137

daily we return, our voices,
which are also your voices, raised,
in anger as in wondering praise,
in the names of the children,
our inheritors, and in your names,
Allison, Jeffrey, Sandra, William,
which are our names also.

*Kent*
*May 4, 1990*

M. L. Liebler

## *The Surface of Murder*

*for Jeff, Allison, Sandy and Bill—With Much Love*

The world can never be
the same after you
have backed into a ghost.
A spirit trapped just
below the surface of murder.

Someday some people will tell
you it never happened,
at least not the way
it was said to have
happened. Death alone.

No place to lie down
and rest itself. Death
that can break your heart
and take with it every
body's dreams and memories.

Cold rain never felt
this lonely, this dark.
And ghosts have never ever
been this close to us,
for if they had, we would

have realized this history
coming long before
we were ever created,
souls seeded with spirit becoming
human, returning back to dust
to be sprinkled below
the surface of murder.

Marvin Bell

## *Green*

We are victims of wars we didn't start
and some we did. We were perpetrators of peace
through inaction, and other times we acted
with results that sliced through air, landing
before falling. We were crowds, larger then,
forming a circle around some absolute point
everyone could see. Shooting at truth,
the marksmen broke our circle. Blood ran then.
It was news where it was left behind.
Once many people regretted, no doubt,
the Boer War. Others followed, regretting
The-War-to-End-All-Wars, then World War Two—
and bad things happened on the homefront, too—
before Korea, Vietnam, Cambodia . . .
Those who couldn't remember the past
found new battles to regret. We gather sometimes
not to remember the wars—but not to forget
the regret. Grief is a long time green.

*Kent State*
*May 4, 1990*

## Paul Metcalf

In a recent letter to me announcing "A Gathering of Poets," Alex Gildzen speaks of "believing that poetry is for remembering and healing." Reading this, I thought at once of the poet Charles Reznikoff, whose two great poems, *Testimony* and *Holocaust*, are classics of just this: remembering and healing.

Writing about *Testimony*, the critic Linda Simon speaks of a passage where Reznikoff forces us "to endure, in yet another line, the long few minutes of suffering before the victim's death. No one, in Reznikoff's world, dies 'instantly.'"

Reznikoff quotes a Chinese poet: " . . . be precise about the thing and reticent about the feeling." Because the sole purpose of the poem is "to convey the feeling."

Be precise and relentless in the remembering—and the feeling—and the healing—will emerge.

Tiff Holland

## *May 4, 1990*

This is the true memorial,
I realized.
The pink cherry blossom sequined raincoat
in front of me all I could see
during the speeches.
This pattern noticed right at the moment
Allison Krause is quoted,
"flowers more important than bullets."
This is the true memorial, I think;
hundreds of colored umbrellas in the rain
like a watercolor I once saw of
Korean women in traditional costume
waiting for a train.
We are waiting for these words
to land like flowers
to color our memorial—
one they can't take away or scale down—
true magnitude,
all these umbrellas, uncovered heads
with rat-drowned hair.
Not even twenty-year anniversary enthusiasm
could keep so many out
in such a cold, cold rain.
It is raining today to keep us honest
in commemoration.
Those here are either pure of heart
or waterproof.
The woman beside me, unknown,
offers to share her umbrella.
I take my turn
keeping it up,
keeping us dry.
When I grasp its handle,
and a cold wind tries to infiltrate beneath,

I suddenly realize what we need to do.
We should join hands,
catch the wind under all the wet domes
and lift off together.
This would be the ultimate statement—
just fly off.
Problem is, I already know
there would be at least one hand hook down
and grab marble, anchor us all.
That's what's going on now.
I don't know that this is wrong.
We are, after all, more rain than air,
and rain falls.
It is important, I think,
to remember the ground.

Elizabeth Mihaly

## *May 4th*

Four students' faces
lie in a limbo land
of gunfire and peace signs
somewhere near a
tree-covered hill
I walk down
after class sometimes.
I don't want to know
their hometowns
or their histories.
Those pictures
in the library
stay with me,
and I think I know
Allison and Bill
and Jeff and Sandy
well enough
to know that
no memorial will
ever be enough,
like an old dead
river bed we
try to fill up.

Steve Posti

## *We Myopic*

It will not be those students, townspeople
professors, guardsmen at Kent State
May 4th 1970
who will write
what history will remember
about that day.
Like lovers,
they hold such different
memories
of the same event.
Each sees May 4th
as the occasion to say
what they believe
needs to be said.
On the Commons
among daffodils
they touch granite
and smell teargas and gunsmoke.
However, history
is not written
with such a fine and intricate typeface.

*April 1990*

Gary Scott

## *Contemplation on Blanket Hill*

For the same reason that
sea gulls are in parking lots
my father is in the mall every morning
with all the walkers all their bad hearts

somewhere between his time and my time
disbelief died
I have never stood anywhere and said I can't believe
this happened I still can't believe this happened I can't
believe this happened here

my father has disbelieved with both sorrow and joy
he is good at it

but what of the slowing of the air
the disturbing heat the heavy water
and what of international banking what of
beauty contests and what of tanning booths

lying perfectly still
watching the clouds
watching the clouds
time is constantly
space is constantly moving past itself like rotation
rotation like movement movement like shopping
movements in and out of shopping malls
my father his jacket over his arm
his shoes his watch his pulse
movements of events
movements in suicide of landslides of ash

disbelief is ash

I feel no disbelief

knowing this world I feel no disbelief in anything
in fact like my father's heart medicine
it seems almost natural

*Kent State*
*May 1990*

Tony Trigilio

## *The Silence of One Hand Clapping*
## *(Kent State University: 1970-1990)*

The army's arrived. The phones
Don't work. Choppers fly above us.
Bayonets shine under a dangerous sun—
                    this spring even
                    the movement
                    of the bees
                    says nothing:
                    no honey
                    no queen


The young woman picks up the phone.
Her girl's at dance class. She wants
To see if the kid is all right—
                    she dials        dials
                    nothing
                    hanging up      she
                    sees wind rustling
                    through the porous air
                    of an Ohio cornfield


A slow fade to black, twenty years
Of credits roll, the dark screen
Silent as a bloodied parking lot—
                    names are titles
                    titles
                    nothing but categories
                    stamps the blind
                    horseman makes us devour
                    at night


148

See the feet, bare feet at dawn,
Nothing to do between trains,
Hard steps near the silent Cuyahoga—

      one pair on the rails
      another
      on the ties  one wading
      the river
      another just
      kicking up stones

Over brown patches of grass steps
Muffled in black-and-white rhythm
Shuffle you forward on your way to class—

      and the plinth
      in the parking lot
      waits like a decayed tooth
      among the flowers
      planted
      each 4th of May

John Sollers

## *Instant Recall*

I remember my home town,
Caldwell, Idaho.
Red, white and blue banners,
"America, Love It or Leave It"
sprouted from fertile Treasure Valley soil.
On May 4, 1970, the hands of a newsprint girl
reached outward and upward
over a body.
On May 4, 1971, I drove into town,
north on Kimball where Panter intersects,
and in the crotch of the Y
the World War II tank sat as always
with its cannon pointed east
in front of the red brick Armory wall.
But from that wall fresh white paint shouted:
REMEMBER KENT STATE.
The porous brick sucked the white enamel deep.
PFCs scrubbed at the white,
but the letters remained.
Then they tried futile chemical douches
and blasts of sand hit the letters
so deep the city engineer cried,
"Structural damage eminent."
Six years later, my four-year-old son
asked, "What's that mean?"
Fifteen years later, they tried red paint,
but it rolled off the white enamel letters
like water beads on a waxed car.

Folks in my home town,
though they weren't there,
though they'd rather not,
still remember.

Alan Williamson

## *Freeze-Frame*

*for the dead at Kent State*

Things stopped: like a freeze-frame, held for twenty years,
though unremembered
when the President tells us to forget that war.

And the Ohio grand jury
would not let your killers
even stand trial . . .

—Is it imaginable they were not
in some way encouraged,
taking aim into the gut of the middle class

only months after a draft lottery
removed two-thirds of it
from any real danger?

So please let us not say
any good came of this,
even if it helped shock us into a world

where Presidents may lie and steal
but not kill more than a handful of our own
in defense of oligarchy . . .

What died here cannot be measured
in the change
from the psychomachias of acid

to the "love yourself" of the self-help books and cocaine . . .
A stunned, slow-witted innocence
spreading, until even language

151

moved, like a numb tool, outside our bodies;
money itself a drug,
the health foods videos exercise machines

a stand-in for lost action—
not a "lost," but a static generation,
waiting for Gorbachev to save the world.

*

What insight that young woman had—
rightly outraging Congress, rightly
softening the people's heart—

to grasp
that this war never rose above the ditch
and is not to be faced

except with a blind, circuitous
half-underworld surprise—
laying the votive cigarettes

and renounced medals
innocently at last
before the blackness-mirror . . .

When they have built one for you
we can go free.

Rosaly DeMaios Roffman

## *Going to Bed Whole:*
## *Kent State Prayer*

**I**

If we could only drink
the dreams of the good world,
kept alive by Mandelstam's wife
saving his poems in her head,
drink the dreams of the world
kept alive by Vincent's brother
sending him his thin undershirts,
drink the dreams of the good world
speaking to us through the round O's
of the sorrows of Goya's soldiers,
we would have the right flags
to fly in undefined battlefields
for the old and desperate young

No, it must be said
four children are not one alone,
they hold the larger field
for the timeless freedom tenderers—
for the strident befores and afters

No, it cannot be said—
        *Remember oh remember*
        *the listless strands of life*
        *hung limp around their eyes*
        *and you cried for them*
        *in the still darkness*
        *such hungry noiseless cries . . .*
no, it cannot be said—
that death did not take us along
though four flowers

are not enough to bargain
villain for villain in time,
and four flowers are superfluous
for the madness of the world
for reaching across forgiveness


## II


I am a mother
A child comes,
says, bring me a world
of my own making
where people are kind
and can understand
the language of beasts
I say
try not to be afraid—

I say
one day you will know
what you must do
to become man or woman—
your life is a distraction from time
your life is a nearness to the earth
No one can say how it will be,
you can try not to be afraid

And if you go out
on the plains—welcome
brothers and sisters,
find ways to draw shelter,
find ways to give strangers food
though they might not understand
why you do what you do

I say
summon those dreams,
put them on shields

I say
make them shine—
those blood jewels

Connie Monson

## *Kent State*

Porch swings, lawns, barbecue pits, maples
and here and there a red trike, careening
from curb to curb, sheepdog bluffing
a low growl. We cruise block after block
on the green expanse of boulevards, watch
the angry lake backing away and storming
forward to the edge of tool-and-dies,
Milwaukee suspended in a cloud of malt.

I think: this can't be home
then remember that tuna casserole evening
I shivered in the leather armchair, staring
at the screen, while a girl, held in a lap, mouth
twisted and moaning, bled to death on television
and I wondered if these children were criminals
or could uniforms be wrong. It was my brother,
not I, who rose from dinner in his quiet sadness,
my father, still eating, not to be moved, confused
by a family he never learned to know.

Two thousand miles away and even now,
in another greening suburb and a life
I pave for myself, that night bothers
like a hangnail, ignored but insistent.
Religion I'd abandoned and saviors
faded like family picture albums
show up again on my nightstand. Someone
holds a block party, and we take turns
talking politics and babysitters over Seagram's
on the rocks. We are children putting up
the badminton net and we divide and rotate
like clockwork and laugh and brush off time
with mosquitoes that come on the evening breeze.

War doesn't touch us here. Still, I name
these people I will never know, the father and son,
the school board member, the woman
with her deaf child, her face open and searching
toward the hills as she turns him to face the sunset.
Now I can feel the damp lake wind and the twining
of my neighbor to neighbor with a bond of cucumber.
I see men and women dance together in the shadows
as though they knew the music, or night, or madness.

Richard Shelton

## *Encounter*

In some small flatland town
a stranger waits for me to arrive by train
and when I step down not knowing
where I am or why I have come
I will recognize him and give him my hand
He will fold my pain like a newspaper
and tuck it under his arm
He will take charge of everything

He will open a car door
I will get in and he will drive
expertly down Main Street out of town
toward open country where the sky
is half the world

As night comes on
we will hear grass beside the road
whispering of its native land
and when the stars bear down like music
I will begin to understand how things
that have never happened before
can happen again

Toi Derricotte

## *For the Dead at Jackson State*

whose names I don't know
because I am as ignorant as newspapers
because I block my ears of so many sounds that
frighten, names I do not call out
names I cannot answer to
that in my heart keep
whispering their syllables

*For Phillip L. Gibbs and James Earl Green*

Kathe Davis

## *The Hardest Thing*

is that there's no undoing it.
Probably every kid who fired
would call his bullet back.
The principled kids facing the guns
would have negotiated, moderated,
they would have talked.
They weren't out to die.
But it can't be undone.

What has always been unbearable
about death is that simple:
it can't be undone.
What has always been unbearable
about time is just
that we move in it one way.

The mother who slaps her child
in a moment of fury knows
her handprint will stay
on his cheek always
under the child skin.

My eleventh grade chemistry teacher
told us irreversibility
was a cooked egg. You can't make
an omelette without breaking eggs,
revolutionaries say, meaning
our children's sweet skulls.

In the poem, Father Williams says, the petal
can be put back on the rose.
In the poem
the dead do live again,

but only as a way
of allowing them to be dead,
allowing us to accept
what is unacceptable.

All the past is present
in the mind, Freud says, and Blake and Hopkins
say nothing is ever lost,
"not a hair is, not an eyelash."
Grownup that you are, you can find
the hurt child you once were
in your head now, and hold
her, hug him, soothe
the terrors, be the parent
to yourself your parents never were.
It is a kind of bootstrap
leverage that is possible, more
amazing than Wall Street
or Frank Lloyd Wright.
Levitation may be possible.
We don't know yet all the mind
can do. We can fix
more than we do.

And you can believe in repair, in healing—we
all have scars, they're
what we share in intimacy—
and still know some reparations
are not possible
even with good glue,
good medicine, good heart.
No unscrambling the egg.
No projector can run
the film backward,
make Jeff Miller's blood reel
back uphill, re-enter his mouth,
his living veins.

The poem shouts no. The heart
cries no. But we
go on hearing gunfire's
echo.

*May 3, 1990*

*VI*

Lisel Mueller

## *Bedtime Story*

The moon lies on the river
like a drop of oil.
The children come to the banks to be healed
of their wounds and bruises.
The fathers who gave them their wounds and bruises
come to be healed of their rage.
The mothers grow lovely; their faces soften,
the birds in their throats awake.
They all stand hand in hand
and the trees around them,
forever on the verge
of becoming one of them,
stop shuddering and speak their first word.

But that is not the beginning.
It is the end of the story,
and before we come to the end,
the mothers and fathers and children
must find their way to the river,
separately, with no one to guide them.
That is the long, pitiless part,
and it will scare you.

Bertolt Brecht

## *On the Infanticide*

## Marie Farrar

**1**

Marie Farrar. Birthdate: April.
No birthmarks, rickets, orphan, underage,
no known previous offenses. Claims
she murdered a baby thus:
she says that in her second month
she went to a woman in a basement apartment,
tried to abort by taking two douches.
Claims they were painful, but didn't work.

*But you, I beg you, don't be angry at her.*
*Each creature needs the help of every other.*


**2**

Nevertheless, she says, she paid what she owed,
and later laced her corset very tight,
also drank kerosene mixed with pepper
though her stomach couldn't hold on to that.
Her belly, visibly swollen, hurt her a lot
and cruelly when she washed the dishes.
At that time, she says, she was still growing.
She prayed to the Virgin Mary, hoped against all hope.

*And you, I beg you, don't be angry at her.*
*Each creature needs the help of every other.*

**3**

But her prayers apparently had no effect.
It was a lot to ask. When she grew bigger
she felt dizzy at morning mass. And she often sweated
from fear, frequently at the altar.
But she kept her condition secret
until the actual time arrived.
Who would believe that someone so plain,
so clumsy, fell victim to temptation?

*And you, I beg you, don't be angry at her.*
*Each creature needs the help of every other.*

**4**

On that day, she says, early in the morning
while washing stairs she felt as if nails
were clawing in her belly. She gets the shivers.
Yet she's able to keep the pain secret.
The whole day hanging out wash
she racks her brains, and then it hits her:
she's about to give birth, and right away
her heart is heavy. But she goes to bed quite late.

*But you, I beg you, don't be angry at her.*
*Each creature needs the help of every other.*

**5**

They woke her up again when she lay in bed:
Snow had fallen and she had to sweep it
till eleven. It was a long day.
But at night she could give birth in peace.
And later she bore, so she says, a son.
The son was a lot like other sons.
She was not a lot like other mothers,
though I have no cause to mock her.

169

*And you, I beg you, don't be angry at her.*
*Each creature needs the help of every other.*

**6**

I'll continue telling
what happened with that son
(she wanted, she says, to conceal nothing)
so that you can see what I am and what you are.
She says she was only in bed a short time
when strong pains struck her, and the only thing
she could think of—not knowing what would happen—
was to force herself not to scream.

*And you, I beg you, don't be angry at her.*
*Each creature needs the help of every other.*

**7**

Then with her last bit of strength, so she says,
since her room had grown ice-cold
she dragged herself to the servants' privy and there—
she doesn't know when exactly—gave birth
quietly. Maybe toward morning. She says
she was now confused, and so numb from cold
because snow could get into the room
that she could hardly hold the baby.

*And you, I beg you, don't be angry at her.*
*Each creature needs the help of every other.*

**8**

Between her room and the privy—before that,
she says, nothing happened—the baby began to cry
and that drove her crazy, she says,
and she hit it blindly with both fists and
couldn't stop until it was still, she says.

170

And then she took the dead thing up with her
to bed for the rest of the night
and in the morning hid it in the washhouse.

*But you, I beg you, don't be angry at her.*
*Each creature needs the help of every other.*

**9**

Marie Farrar. Birthdate: April.
Died in the penitentiary at Meissen,
unmarried mother, condemned, showing
the weakness of all creatures—
You who give birth in nice clean sheets,
you who call your impregnated bellies "blessed"
don't damn people lost and powerless;
if their sins were great, great also were their sorrows.

*So, I beg you, don't be angry at her.*
*Each creature needs the help of every other.*

*translated by Ed Ochester*

Kelly Cherry

## *The Fate of the Children*

*Abraham reads the entrails of the ram and foretells the future.*

Lately, in Cambodia, they tear the children apart.
What Solomon only threatened, they make real.
One soldier grabs an arm,
another a leg.

Meanwhile, in Czechoslovakia,
the children are prevented from living with their parents, refugees.
Reunification of this family is "in contradiction with the interests of
    the socialist state."

In Russia, little girls wear white bows in their hair;
gauze butterflies perch on their blonde or brunette curls.
If their parents object to the lack of civil liberty, or, say, simply to
    the sudden disappearance of a dear friend,
the little girls pay for their fathers' "sins."
(And the fathers pay also, and the mothers.)
The little girls are pinned to their places like butterflies in glass
    cases.

Then again, according to eyewitnesses,
Lieutenant Calley tore an infant from the arms of a Buddhist priest,
tossing it into the air like a clay pigeon,
and shot it forever dead with his army-issue M-16.

None of this is poetry; it is fact.
And not only fact, but act.
And not only act, but raw fat and warm blood, hope expiring
like breath, and shadow
beating a menacing tattoo on the wall of the house in a high wind,
    like an overgrown bush,

and I refuse to pretend it is poetry,
seeing it is not even food.

Lord, Lord . . . what is poetic about the way we slaughter our
    children,
the way we sacrifice our sons
like lambs,
yes, precisely:  like lambs?

Kevin Clark

## *The Sky*

> . . . *let a whole moment move through you*
> *without the fear of being cruel . . .*
> —*Honor Moore, "Poem for the End"*

Two ten year old boys hold a third
younger boy to a tree, and say
words I no longer remember saying.
The pinned boy struggles, then
shakes his head "No," the older boys
each in turn slapping his face
lightly, then harder. They laugh,
they spit in his face, and the younger boy

looks up through the heavy branches,
the morning's leaves. He is too young
to know why the sky disturbs him, its
new and irresilient blue, why he shuts
his eyes and takes in its hard distance,
the others—for a small moment—nearly

gone. Finally, a sharp slap pulls him
back, and he begins to cry. When we let him
go, he only sits there, refusing
his mother's refuge, and that afternoon
or the next, a change has come,
and the three of us all send
toy cavalries across the Plains,
torching the teepees, dying
over and over in each other's arms.

All yesterday Harry Stanley's face
stared at me from the newspaper
like a memory, though I'd never
heard of the man who refused
Lieutenant Calley's orders to shoot
the people in the pit. I'm forty and
can seem so far from such a history.
Yet the late afternoon Pacific sky
wants to lower its hard white haze
onto the shoulders of my four-year-old
who calls and digs in the sand just beyond
the surf's reach. I jerk at every step
he takes toward the blue teeth of the waves.
Harry Stanley grew up on another coast,
eating greens and catfish beneath
a genial sky. He still can't believe
they served spaghetti on the night
his prayers fell like mist. Now
he's back home alone, plays chess
with his one friend, speaks few words.
There are days he dare not look up.

*

The haze descends, then hovers. I hope
for one permanent, soft word
to take us all back. My father, too,
was a good man, but my young brother
once bolted down the muddy road from him
for fear of the hard tones. Now I imagine
in the horizonless distance the field
where my son may first love his own harsh
will, the opposing catcher turned
for the throw, and my son, so delightfully
free, a blue fire, hurtling shoulder-first
into the soft meat of the boy's kidney,
the ball a blur to the backstop.

175

He may remember this moment with mixed
pleasure, sitting on a beach, middle-aged
and conscious of more than the perfect
collision:  a new absence he'll try
to dissolve like light in a water cup.

*

I remember the air laughing in kindly
octaves. It is my father rewarding
one of Glenn's jokes, a silliness.
We have this secret with my father:
we're all boys. And when my mother
over dishes turns angry at our play,

we slip out with him, telling him
our stories, how we'd leapt skyward
all afternoon like long jumpers
to land hard on the back half
of caterpillars, measuring how far
the green intestines shot
down the sidewalk, my father
caterwauling in feigned disgust,
and telling us the comic stories
of his New York childhood, his voice
lifting us into the altitudes of dusk,
the old Chevy floating nose up. Then

why don't I remember what it was Glenn did
on a spring day that so quickly shred
the air's wing? How long did he fall
that one time, my father having caught
and thrown him down into the new brutal sky,
before he hit the roadside without a sound?

My son runs up to the blanket and swats
his plastic bat at the sand. It's absurd
to think of both Harry Stanley at Mai Lai
and my father playing in the fastpitch
softball league at home, the off-duty cop
swearing from the mound at Fantry the ump,
who pulls off his facemask, steps redfaced
out to the infield, screaming, c'mon, Murph,
right here, right now, you sonofabitch,
and then my father's face as he looks at me
from the on-deck circle, the way he wants
to smile but can only shake his head and
gaze at my face, studying it as if he'd lost
me. My son is trying to pound sand beetles
which are too quick for him, then points
at a seagull. I point up with him

as perhaps one of the fathers in the pit
with his son in his arms pointed up
to a cloud in the blue sky, urging him
in the softest voice to study it.
At that very moment the lieutenant measured
Harry Stanley's eyes, and ordered him to fire.
Only months ago in Mississippi the corporal
had seen in the morning sky something
fragile:  as if prayer were made of colors
that would dissolve when the words were spoken.
In a clear, low tone he told Calley,
no. Then, when the rifles began
repeating their ecstatic word
out of the sky, he memorized the parent's
last sounds. Hours later, he turned from
the unbearable dinner, and stared
into the colorless sky of his water cup.

At forty my son may come to this beach
to show his own boy how to hit,
describe the liquid smack of bat on ball,
to stand behind him, molding the tiny hands
around the bat, all four hands lashing
the air with practice swings, then to say,
yes, good, good, and to cup his cheek
in a rough right hand for as long
as he'll let him, to nod and smile. My son may
have learned by then it's not the wrath
of skin against skin, not even the knuckles
of the upward right hand entering
the lacery behind a cheekbone, the drunken
patrons hooting, the bartender at once
grabbing his sawed-off cue stick
and bawling for an end to it. He may
have remembered the one blissful sentence
he spoke to his stunned father, each word
a step into the new life he'd thought
a man must need to live, each incremental
expression on his father's face crossing
a sky of lives, all solitary, all
earned on the cold defiant wind
blown like fast blood out of the heart.

But that wind is not a life, and if
at forty my son comes to this beach
and recalls the bloodless weight
of his younger heart, he may need help
against the insistent version of a sky
that becomes stone. To move
a whole moment through that stone
without the fear of being cruel
he will need his father, and

he will only have him if, at that
brute moment when his cold male
sentence bore the shot space
between us, I, like Harry Stanley,
had moved motionless through the old
impulse, had found one unpetrified
word to hold quietly, as I would
quietly hold open a door for a friend
who may freely choose to leave, or to stay.

*May 1990*

Leasa Burton

## *Maud Harris*

*In 1931, when jockey Willie Shoemaker was born
prematurely, no one expected him to live. According
to legend, his grandmother placed him in an oven
overnight, hoping the warmth would keep him alive.*

Mother now midwife to daughter
holding the baby away from the body
first to see blood and placenta
wrapped loosely around bone
half flesh, half wire
a boy born so light he could not harness air.
She cut the cord
could not hold him or send him
back to that moment before he knew
his mother or grandmother, the light
of the oven in the kitchen she loved
how the linoleum yellowed a path from sink and counter
to oven then table, and she the middle
the eye that whispered "Willie Shoemaker."
She saw the words grow warm
condense on the window
knew he might not live, she
searched her closet, winter wool coat
Sunday shoes, out of the box
cardboard smelling like leather
she lit the oven, left open the door
him inside
loaf of bread to rise.

Jeanne Bryner

## *Arrows*

My brother tells me deer are too plentiful and will surely starve in a hard winter. He kills them with his curved bow and long rifle.

My brother has blue eyes and he will teach his blue-eyed sons the ways of killing; how the hunter must be quiet and wait in tree stands. How deer will not always die quickly, but will run through wire fences, sometimes small creeks; their blood splashing on leaves, dropping on rotting limbs. They leave a trail.

My brother will tell his sons, "The shot should be clear. It is wrong to leave the wounded in the forest."

Cornstalks will swell and lie broken. Wars will come and boys will be called. Steaming gasps will rise like ghost dancers in the forest and young boys will not always die quickly. My brother will run through wire fences, his tears, small creeks, his warm blood splashing here and there. His sons' blue eyes will arrow-pierce his heart.

Jill Moses

## "Child with a toy hand grenade in Central Park, N.Y.C."

*after a photograph by Diane Arbus*

You stand on the clay battlefield in your Keds,
one hand and mouth contorted into pain
beyond your years,
the other hand squeezing the grenade
to crush the faces in the park.
What explodes is only summer light.
At night, child, you dream of fingers that point,
fists that clench in schoolyards,
muskets, cannons, rifles, and blades.
You lose your boyish heap:
marbles of agate, jacks, cat's cradle string.

From a balcony, my nephew shoots bathers with a cap gun,
and mimics the action of stretching a bow
then becomes a sheriff with holster and badge.
Every game has its weapon and range,
every target has a face.
He is James Bond, Robocop, a Ghostbuster
who makes the enemy disintegrate.
He doesn't know words like *draft*, *Nam*, *Laos*.
He doesn't know his father's numbers: 52, 1-Y, 4-F
and how the wings of geese burst toward Canada.

Patricia Goedicke

## *Dead Baby*

In the kitchen I open the spoon drawer
     with a yank and a dead baby's head falls out,
  don't tell me it doesn't happen it does,
    my shrink tells me don't pay any attention to it,
       of course nobody *wants*
         to let the potato rot,
    but once it's been pulled from the ground
         and sent, gasping, on its way
  a spoon's only a spoon
      for stirring beets, pickled
    with thick sugar for sweet
   peaceful lovemaking

Except that the knife's always after it! *L'chaim*
    we say but watch out for the bath water,
        my shrink tells me strange things
  will be found there,
    lives nobody wanted
       even enough to think about for one
   quick second before fattening them up
    nine months in the oven,
   then dropping them
    like plates on somebody else's doorstep,

With nothing to protect them from guns, contras
    and counter-contras, !?!*Rambo*!?!
  and James !?!*Bond*!?!, everything's greasier
 and redder nowadays, my shrink tells me
    it's not your business but I can't
  even go to the movies anymore
     without being run over by a speeding
   truck, motorboat, nuclear
    sinister submarine, its underside
     slides across my face with shark venom

183

underslung teeth like tank treads
in 3-D dripping their vile bodily discharges
all over me as the murderously
athletic spy's high flying kick leaps

Right at me! Ketchupy
red blood squirts
at the exact center of my sexiest
best skirt, O why is !?!*Fuck*!?!
such a four letter word when it feels so
!?!*nice*!?!, all it wants
in the long run is healthy
well-fed babies to grow up
quietly, waving their rosy arms
like soup spoons at the ballot boxes,

So why do they call lovemaking ?!?*names*!?!
the hatred they run the world with
gurgles up in me like ink,
as my arteries hiss and pop,
I who only wanted to cook
a few meals for the family,
my shrink tells me you don't *have* to be a victim,
all this violence
in books, at the movies, is just
repressed helplessness,
rage everyone should express
before we act it out, he says

But everyday when the fire sweaty Stealth
disgusting bomber and the lying
congressional pig-on-the-take ramps over
my living room rug,
as the garbage gets taken out
sloppier and sloppier,
as the green plastic body bags
keep ripping, though the fury I feel at the state
of all these squash-everyone's-true-feelings, patriotic
invasions of small countries

184

may be only a childish longing
somehow to get back to my real parents
George and Martha Washington, my shrink tells me
history's infinitely disposable,
kids make these things up
all the time, the lewd
uncle in the closet, mom
casually looking on, the napalm,

Even the poisonousness of powdered milk
for the Third World's mostly a Grimms' fairy tale
he tells me, especially for those who know
which drawers to keep shut,
the head rolling across the linoleum's
just an accident, the boat people
eating and being eaten,
the newest rash of cancerous
scaly skin blotches proliferating,
the blisters on young trees, all the water
underground tables turned
rustier every day, he insists
such nightmares are pure knee-jerk
liberal poppycock, nothing but an excuse
for not thinking about your own problems
which are *really* serious,
see what a long way you've come
even in this poem from thinking about the starved, chopped up
dead baby.

Chana Bloch

## *Rising To Meet It*

Pain is the salty element.

All that night I lay
tethered to my breathing. To the pain,
the fixed clock-stare of the walls,
the fingers
combing my tangled hair.
Ride out the waves, the doctor said.

The first time I touched a man,
what startled me more than the pleasure
was knowing what to do.
I turned to him with
a motion so firm it must have been
forming inside me
before I was born.

I was swimming upstream, the body
solid, bucking for breath, slippery,
wet. An ocean
rolled off my shoulders.

Tonight, strapped to the long night, I miss
the simple
pain of childbirth—
                                    No, not the pain
but that rising to meet it like a body
reaching out in desire, buoyant, athletic,
sure of its power.

Galway Kinnell

## *The Olive Wood Fire*

When Fergus woke crying at night
I would carry him from his crib
to the rocking chair and sit holding him
before the fire of thousand-year-old olive wood,
which it took a quarter-hour of matches
and kindling to get burning right. Sometimes
—for reasons I never knew and he has forgotten—
even after his bottle the big tears
would keep on rolling down his big cheeks
—the left cheek always more brilliant than the right—
and we would sit, some nights for hours,
rocking in the almost lightless light
eking itself out of the ancient wood,
and hold each other against the darkness,
his close behind and far away in the future,
mine I imagined all around.
One such time, fallen half-asleep myself,
I thought I heard a scream
—a flier crying out in horror
as he dropped fire on he didn't know what or whom,
or else a child thus set aflame—
and sat up alert. The olive wood fire
had burned low. In my arms lay Fergus,
fast asleep, left cheek glowing, God.

Maggie Anderson

## *Heart Fire*

*In memory of Aaron Goodman*
*(1962–1983)*

Three months since your young son shot himself
and, of course, no one knows why. It was October.
Maybe he was following the smell of dying leaves
or the warmth of the fire in the heart, so hard
to locate in a country always readying for war.

One afternoon we sat together on your floor, drinking
tea and listening to Brahms on the radio. He would
have liked this music, you told me. He would have liked
everything I like now and what he wouldn't like I don't
like either. He has made the whole world look like him.

Today, driving into Pittsburgh, I see you are right.
The sky is cold blue like a shirt I once saw him
wear and the bare trees are dark, like his hair.
I see how vulnerable the grasses are, pale and flimsy
by the roadsides, trying to stand straight in the wind.

At Canonsburg, all the pink and green and purple houses
have the same slant of roof toward the hill, like toys
because I'm thinking about children, how sometimes
we want to give them up if they seem odd and distant,
yet even if they die before us, we cannot let them go.

I see your son in landscapes as I drive, in a twist
of light behind a barn before the suburbs start,
or under a suburban street light where a tall boy
with a basketball has limbs like those he had just
outgrown. Because I want to think he's not alone,

I invent for him a heart fire even the unenlightened
living are sometimes allowed to see. It burns past
the white fluorescence of the city, past the steel mills
working off and on as they tell us we need, or don't
need, heavy industry for fuel, or war. Your son

keeps me company, driving down the last hill into
Pittsburgh, in the tunnel as I push for good position
in the lanes. He is with me as I spot the shiny cables
of the bridge and gear down, as all the lights beyond
the river come on now, across his safe, perfected face.

Lori Jakiela

## *"Sometimes I See Angels"*

*—Dr. Elisabeth Kübler-Ross*

Children, she says, know death
better than they know what it means
to color inside the lines. "They know
but they're not afraid. They want us
not to be afraid," she says, looking
at her hands as if they were not her hands,
at construction-paper stars and pictures
taken from refrigerators, mirrors,
bedroom walls. In her home, children

are dying of AIDS and she helps them
paint what matters:  black dogs,
green summer castles on yellow hills,
stick angels with purple hair,
red smile sunsets.

She remembers when she was young, how
she went to Maidanek, a visitor
"It's different to read a book
about Anne Frank, but smell the furnaces,
see cartloads of small shoes, women's hair,
the children's barracks filled with butterflies
scratched into wood with their fingernails."
Fear, she says, is what makes us hate.

Neighbors line her driveway with nails and glass,
the ambulance, the police won't come.
"They hold their breath
when they drive past. They're afraid
it's in the air, that it's growing
in children's tears."
At town meetings there are protests,

190

petitions. They want guarantees—
that real estate prices
will not go down,
that attendance at the Maple Festival
will not go down. She has no

guarantees, doesn't understand, these are
good people, she says, Christians. She asks
if Jesus took care of lepers, why can't she
care for children? One woman stands,
shouts, "But you aren't Jesus."

Charles Rossiter

## *Daddy, What Color is Thunder*

*For Erika  May 4, 1970—August 7, 1989*

And you were there, in the wrong place
at the wrong time, innocent, midday,
on a familiar two lane road and probably
singing along with the radio

Erika, I see you everywhere, in the mirror,
my eyes are your eyes, my body—
the body you once had, now ashes
in the sea. Be still, daughter,
the tides will take you

You will know the color of thunder.

Kate Daniels

## from *The Niobe Poems*

### The Little King

He rode to bed that last night
on a throne of arms,
the seat of his pants
sticky with pine tar,
an overgrown zucchini
standing in for a sceptre.

Were the gods watching
even then? Were they saying,
that's him, that's the one
we want, the one
we get to have
because we're strong enough
to take him,
because we do not care
about the mortal mother
he'll leave behind,
her wailing, her wild
weeping, the pills
she'll have to take to sleep,
her strong and suffocating wish
to throw herself after him
into the earth, as if he were a god
himself, who had punished her
by taking away all she lived for,
every single thing she loved.

## The Gods Are Optional

The gods sat in the trees
that evening, green and darkening,
lingering over a last coffee,
coffee with a shot of rum.
The river was talking to them
but they were gods and didn't have
to listen. Even in the trees
it was hot that night. The leaves were not
delightful as they knew how to be.
The gods stirred in the trees, they looked
away. The river was talking
to them more urgently. "I don't
want this," it said. "I don't need it."
But the gods had worked enough
that day. And the evening
was so hot the little mortal
flung himself into the water.

Inside the house beside the river,
someone talked on the telephone.
Someone wrote in a notebook.
The windows were just openings
no one happened to look through.
The hands on the clock lurched forward forever.

# Afterwards Apollo

Walked around in the dark woods,
shaking his head, his bow loose
in his nervous hand.
He wasn't sure what had happened,
why there had been all that blood
and the piteous wailing.
And why it had been
his job, anyway,
to murder children.

If you could have seen him then
illuminated from within
by the force of his thinking
like an ancient tree ignited
for a moment by a lightning bolt,
would he have seemed magnanimous,
as in the legend, or only humanly
confused? The huge wooden branches
groaning and glistening with light
in the dark. The two feelings
fighting in him, and not
being able to tell, ever,
which one would win.

## But Artemis

Was less uncertain than her brother.
She lay down in her favorite wood
and licked her privates and watched
the night grow darker. She could hear
Apollo pacing through the woods,
working it out. She laughed
a low, contented laugh and threaded
her fingers through her pubic hair.
She needed this every now and then.
She liked it
when they recognized her fatal form
and understood her hunter's task.
The screams only wakened something
harder and more
untouchable in her. And *then*
it really was almost
sexual:  great, winglike fans
rising inside, a low fire
in her groin, her nipples standing out
taut and black.

She was never sorry afterwards,
or tortured by ambiguity.
There was a reason somewhere
but that was not
her job. Because she
was a god.
She laughed, watching
them rage at her,
at the way they couldn't stop
hating her. Didn't they know
after all this time?
Didn't they see
there was nothing
any of them could do to her.
She kept on floating above them,

lovely and terrible,
but still somehow
desirable.

# The Death of the Niobids

Afterwards it was very still.
For a short while
they lay there alone
and no one knew
what had happened.
The sun beat down
on the broken bodies.
The silver arrows glittered
in the summer light.

If you had come upon it
would you have believed
what you saw? The country
at peace but the family
slaughtered at the municipal park.

Would you have shaken your head
and hurried on, disbelieving?
Or would you have been the one
who went on to the palace
after covering the bodies,
the one who had to tell Niobe,
who placed his hands on her shoulders
that were turned to glass
and forced her down into a chair
and brought the sip of water.
Were you the one, then,
who told her to submit
and advised her to accept
whatever the gods dished out?

Then it was you
she came to afterwards,
standing in your preacher's frock.

After the funeral.
After the mourning.
After the rock.
You were the one
she looked in the face
and told to fuck off.

Maj Ragain

## *The Children Jump Over the Trenches*

Off my back step,
I try to sort through what is there,
the tulip tree, the white clover,
the concrete, the puddle leached by heat,
the bricks in patterns
that someone thought made sense.

The children tumble in, breathless,
kicking up the air in pinks and purples.
My seven year old daughter,
the neighbor girls, a scraped knee,
bandaids.
They ride their bikes down their driveway
and into the street.
The little wound is pedaled away.

I sit here with this poem,
trying to make it come loose,
listening for the creak of a bicycle wheel,
waiting for the children.
They do come back, hungry
and thirsty,
quarreling without rancor.
Where did they learn to write
in the air with their mouths?

You know when the fathers built this town,
they first laid out a gridwork of trenches.
Someone had to dig them,
so the fathers advertised
in the newspapers of distant cities
for men without families
to come dig.
When the trenches were finished

and the pipes and the cable laid in them,
the workers were made to surrender
their clothing
and their faces were painted.
Each man was asked to kneel
in an open trench named the Mainline.
Each man was shot once
in the back of the head.

All of this was covered with top soil
and green sod carpet unrolled over it.
The one man who would not submit
was caught within the hour,
hiding in the trees,
still trusting that
the children would find him first.

*VII*

Rita Dove

## *"Teach Us to Number Our Days"*

In the old neighborhood, each funeral parlor
is more elaborate than the last.
The alleys smell of cops, pistols bumping their thighs,
each chamber steeled with a slim blue bullet.

Low-rent balconies stacked to the sky.
A boy plays tic-tac-toe on a moon
crossed by tv antennae, dreams

he has swallowed a blue bean.
It takes root in his gut, sprouts
and twines upward, the vines curling
around the sockets and locking them shut.

And this sky, knotting like a dark tie?
The patroller, disinterested, holds all the beans.

August. The mums nod past, each a prickly heart on a sleeve.

Louise McNeill

## *The Grave Creek Inscribed Stone*

The stone tablet they found in the mound at Grave Creek,
With hieroglyphics or mystic runes carved there on its face as the
    copy shows it,
But the stone itself long stolen away—
Or broken—lost—
What words did it say?
Query the query forever.

Of a noble Adena king,
Of his wars, his conquest?

Or of sky-gods riding on white wings out of the west?
Or did it tell how to plant pumpkins, squashes, sunflower?

Or of that strange death-pox that swept the village,
Fever and black buboes and rotting bone?
Then, at the last, this one slow-dying scholar
Carving his terror inward on the stone.

Or of how copper is melted, where the copper veins run in the rock
    face beside the Lake of Winds?

Or did some old seer, mask-faced and gray, medicine man of all
    strong medicine, carve in fading eye-light
His one last message to the Earth?

*Make no war among you.*
*Brother to brother speak before the long silence swells your tongue.*
*Offer work and seed to the One Only.*
*Drink not from the gourd of your in-laws.*
*Touch not your footsoles to the moon.*
*Joy in your hour of sunlight.*
*Endure evil.*
*Beware the atom when it comes.*

Irene McKinney

## *Visiting My Gravesite:*
## *Talbott Churchyard, West Virginia*

Maybe because I was married and felt secure and dead
at once, I listened to my father's urgings about "the future"

and bought this double plot on the hillside with a view
of the bare white church, the old elms, and the creek below.

I plan now to use both plots, luxuriantly spreading out
in the middle of a big double bed. —But no,

finally, my burial has nothing to do with my marriage, this lying
    here
in these same bones will be as real as anything I can imagine

for who I'll be then, as real as anything undergone, going back
and forth to "the world" out there, and here to this one spot

on earth I really know. Once I came in fast and low
in a little plane and when I looked down at the church,

the trees I've felt with my hands, the neighbors' houses
and the family farm, and I saw how tiny what I loved or knew was,

it was like my children going on with their plans and griefs
at a distance and nothing I could do about it. But I wanted

to reach down and pat it, while letting it know
I wouldn't interfere for the world, the world being

everything this isn't, this unknown buried in the known.

Jan Beatty

## *Asking the Dead for Help*

The horses are standing still now,
droop-backed and silent in silver stalls.
I think they are dead, not asleep.
I think they are mourning the world,
their manes hanging sadly on their necks
like someone else's unwashed hair.
Here in this pine-filled valley
there is no relief from the still life.
I see myself, other humans standing
motionless in their stalls, silent in the valley,
breathing the dust, now and then
sucking the air for something new.

I visit my father's grave and stare at the aging spruce,
wondering what it is we say when there's nothing to lose.
I want to hear the final breath of the living,
all of a man's life condensed to a sigh,
the words uttered at the moment between worlds,
the only words that can save us.

Dahlia Ravikovitch

## *Hovering at a Low Altitude*

I am not here.
I am on those craggy eastern hills
streaked with ice,
where grass doesn't grow
and a wide shadow lies over the slope.
A shepherd girl appears
from an invisible tent,
leading a herd of black goats to pasture.
She won't live out the day,
that girl.

I am not here.
From the deep mountain gorge
a red globe floats up,
not yet a sun.
A patch of frost, reddish, inflamed,
flickers inside the gorge.

The girl gets up early to go to the pasture.
She doesn't walk with neck outstretched
and wanton glances.
She doesn't ask, Whence cometh my help.

I am not here.
I've been in the mountains many days now.
The light will not burn me, the frost
won't touch me.
Why be astonished now?
I've seen worse things in my life.

I gather my skirt and hover
very close to the ground.
What is she thinking, that girl?
Wild to look at, unwashed.

For a moment she crouches down,
her cheeks flushed,
frostbite on the back of her hands.
She seems distracted, but no,
she's alert.

She still has a few hours left,
but that's not what I'm thinking about.
My thoughts cushion me gently, comfortably.
I've found a very simple method,
not with my feet on the ground, and not flying—
hovering
at a low altitude.

Then at noon,
many hours after sunrise,
that man goes up the mountain.
He looks innocent enough.
The girl is right there,
no one else around.
And if she runs for cover, or cries out—
there's no place to hide in the mountains.

I am not here.
I'm above those jagged mountain ranges
in the farthest reaches of the east.
No need to elaborate.
With one strong push I can hover and whirl around
with the speed of the wind.
I can get away and say to myself:
I haven't seen a thing.
And the girl, her palate is dry as a potsherd,
her eyes bulge,
when that hand closes over her hair, grasping it
without a shred of pity.

*translated by Chana Bloch*
*and Ariel Bloch*

Toi Derricotte

## *Captivity:  The Minks*

In the backyard of our house on Norwood,
there were five hundred steel cages lined up,
each with a wooden box
roofed with tar paper;
inside, two stories, with straw
for a bed. Sometimes the minks would pace
back and forth wildly, looking for a way out;
or else they'd hide in their wooden houses, even when
we'd put the offering of raw horse meat on their trays, as if
they knew they were beautiful
and wanted to deprive us.
In spring the placid kits
drank with glazed eyes.
Sometimes the mothers would go mad
and snap their necks.
My uncle would lift the roof like a god
who might lift our roof, look down on us
and take us out to safety.
Sometimes one would escape.
He would go down on his hands and knees,
aiming a flashlight like
a bullet of light, hoping to catch
the orange gold of its eyes.
He wore huge boots, gloves
so thick their little teeth couldn't bite through.
"They're wild," he'd say. "Never trust them."
Each afternoon when I put the scoop of raw meat rich
with eggs and vitamins on their trays,
I'd call to each a greeting.
Their small thin faces would follow as if slightly curious.
In fall they went out in a van, returning
sorted, matched, their skins hanging down on huge metal
hangers, pinned by their mouths.
My uncle would take them out when company came

and drape them over his arm—the sweetest cargo—
He'd blow down the pelts softly
and the hairs would part for his breath
and show the shining underlife which, like
the shining of the soul, gives us each
character and beauty.

C. D. Wright

## *The Legend of Hell*

*homage to Barbara McClintock*

A few hours ago a woman went on a walk.
Her phone rang and rang.
What a pleasure, she said to herself,
To walk in the fields and pick walnuts.

A moment ago a white dog
whose chain snared a shopping cart,
barked and barked.
Someone sauntered through an orchard
with murdering the whole family on his mind.

At the Black Pearl dancing was nightly.
That Sonnyman showed up again,
too tall for his clothes.
The pretentious copper beech threw its final shadow
on the D.A.'s house. Where we were living,
you wouldn't dream of going unaccompanied.

A few hours ago you could be at the movies,
borrow a comb from a stranger.
In the cities you had your braille libraries;
couples dining on crustacean
with precious instruments. In the provinces
you had your jug bands, Anabaptists sharing their yield.

Then comes the wolf:
in a room of a house on a plain
lie the remains of Great Aunt Gladys
the quintessential Bell operator
sent many a rose by many a party in pain.

(By remains, we mean depression
left by her big body on her high bed);
over here we have an early evening scene without figures,
the soft parts of children blown into trees.
Our neighbors are putting on their prettiest things.
Their clocks have stopped but all hearts calibrated.

They say they are ready now
to make their ascension into light.
And you Edward Teller we know you're out there
shelling nuts; saying to yourself alone,
Now this is a pleasure.

Edward Field

## *The Reprieve*

Away for a month, I knew something was missing,
but just couldn't put my finger on it.
Why should I feel confused in this foreign city,
so clean and orderly after New York, so safe,
so civilized? Instead, I'm like one of those writers
ransomed from the Nazis—one day the concentration camp,
the next Hollywood, lounging by a swimming pool
under palm trees in the sun,
where the nightmare is still the reality.

In this city of no roaches, I'm sickened by the memory
of what I'll soon be going back to, the exploding
bug population, part of daily life there,
among all the problems in the world,
surely not the greatest, I try to tell myself—where,
still vulnerable from dreams, with your morning hard-on,
to have to start swatting them
around the kitchen sink, the counter . . . .
In fear, they panic,
and you are the whips, the dogs,
the barking commands, the blinding lights,
and in the confusion, how hard they run,
for life is sweet to them.

Lynn Wikle

## *Three Lakes, Wisconsin*

We were kids, driving home
two hours late after parking
in the birches behind the garbage pits
where the bears came to feed
when we found the overturned Chevy
and the man tossed backwards in the ditch.

We smoked our Winstons
and waited to flag down the next car.
The man was already dead.
Would it work to tell my mother
we waited three hours?
I dragged my skirt in his blood.
Then we drove home,
drinking the rest of his beer
and practicing my story.

Thirty years later I'm home for a week,
helping Mother get ready to die.
We're at the kitchen table, sorting snapshots
when she tells me, "You were always
the bad one, the one who lied."

I go outside to smoke a cigarette.
I am not the good daughter.
I am the one who stole, who stayed out late,
the smoky-smelling one, jaggy as
a broken light bulb, here on the porch,
shut out of my mother's house, telling lies.

Judith Rachel Platz

## *Crossing*

But
I remember
the meadow insects
their tiny world
a heady exhilaration
and in thick morning mist
I rolled down hillsides
the tall grass a green coat
that warmed my body's cold.
I remember
catching butterflies
in my small hand
to hold for awhile
and then let go.

You can see more clearly
looking down on it all.
It is like slow motion
and it exaggerates
to be *in* it.
There is a membrane
between.
You watch for awhile,
then let go.

Judy Lindberg

## *Three Steel Mill Pins*

There's one for each decade my father
worked at the mill in revolving shifts,
seven to three, three to eleven, eleven to seven,
coming and leaving through our kitchen door,
in and out of my days, my head turning at the click
of our door knob, watching his hair turn from curly black
to straight silver.
Coming home in oily boots and twill work clothes
to potato sausage and eggs and us.
Leaving again, the Big Depression words of his youth
were bulldozers pushing him to overtime
and time and a half and vacations spent painting the house,
until the chest pains started
and the company doctor wouldn't let him go back to work
and he swore we'd lose everything and his heart froze.
When we sorted his things, giving some away,
I took these pins and twirled them in my fingers,
bronze, silver, gold, the last one
still wrapped in cellophane.
Each one a wreath circling a torch,
with thirty years hanging in the empty space
between laurel leaf and flame.

Todd Moore

## *i've never told*

anyone abt being
a dillinger
hostage til now
i remember the
wind it was
so cold standing
on that running
board dillinger
was driving he
kept looking
over to see if
i was still
there what cd
i do at 60 miles
an hour the
road went under
the car too
fast & i was
afraid to look
down even to
see if my legs
were still
there i was
ready to die
& didn't expect
the hundred
dollar bill
dillinger shoved
into my hand
i was afraid to
spend the money
so i hid it

in the bible
at the 23rd
psalm

Tom Beckett

## *Specific Nouns*

This is this

intersection.

I want to put

my pain into

the window.

I'd cut my

penis off

but it

has taken

so long

to grow fuzzy

squishy, soft

and bumpy

lumpy, doughy.

I am shy

I am pro-noun

but not my poetry.

So, between waking

and sleeping, between

eye and window

framed, blended, bleached

reconciled, remarked

marketed, marked

down, made, retailed

it is said.

Close-up of any part

of *any* body.


I don't respect

the way I expect you

to behave.

The President may not

be well liked but

he is well armed.


I've had the tonic.

Is there a *dominant*

water, too?

Exercise caution

as you approach

or else

altogether avoid

wet spot poetics.

Little pornographic

allegories

fuel fucking

speed conception.

Reception

theories puddle

in the middle

of a hotbed

of radicals.

Repetition

is a form

of zucchini.

I'd rather catch.

I am in

-articulate

most of the time.


I want you

to include me

in an image

of how I feel.


Outlined solids.

Outlying solidarities.


Don't stand outside

our exteriority.

Fuck me inside

these consuming

realities.


Give me my head.

Specific nouns

refused

at the doors

of perception

are later returned

on the backs

of great verbs

of burden

confused by

difference and

opposition (confused

by what *separates*

difference

and opposition).


Where are we

in this?

Brooke Horvath

## *A Matter of Trees*

Sometimes it's just the sound of words
& their positions on the page, read
with a quiet violence, leaving a stain behind.
As when the weather turned cold
and the black walnuts fell, how
we gathered them, grandfather and I,
our fingers dyed brown and browner,
how one time we entered a field
the theme of which was sheep,
some dead (some dog) some not.
It was upon the dead the accent fell,
the magical horror—a matter of trees
and windy silence like the sound of Ohs
and the odd positioning of bodies,
like the exact word in the right place,
each walnut in its place, its place
the grass, now the basket,
bringing them home for squirrels
to winter on. Buried them mostly,
the squirrels did, as farmers
their sheep—or whatever farmers do
with sheep the dog has ravaged,
leaving their eyes like blank verse,
the dog returning later to the field
to scan a line of scarecrow trees.

Thomas Meyer

## *The Desert*

Today we went further before the sun
came up but stopped by what appeared
to be nine or ten a.m. to rest.

I lay my head in your arms, confused
by the events of the last three (maybe
four) days . . . the Indian we found
who took us to water, then ran away

leaving us there . . . Your leg healed
somewhat, enough, at least, to walk on,
and when you tire I hold you in my arms:
we dance across the sand.

Nothing else moves. We hardly speak:
throats too dry. We try to go at night
by stars. Even so, only this scorching

sun allows us true directions.

Sophie Crawford

## *Inland Sea*

Inland, looking into the canyon
we dream our bodies
like the fish floating in rocks,
sink with the sea and
are empty.
Maybe the moon tilted,
the canyon sucked in
its belly of water. Now is the rasp
of sand, green husk,
brown crust, crumbling boulders,
tundra, the long swells of earth
reaching down.

We can't move our legs,
raise our hands.
Blind, we can't stop our eyes
from rolling back.
The nurses at St. Cecilia's Hospital
who lift our hands,
rub our legs are speechless
and ample, night-limbed.
It's given
we have never loved ourselves
but these women press
half their lives into our muscles
and nerves, into our blood.

They bend our knees
one by one and together,
stretch our thin arms
over our heads, arching our backs,
forcing vowels from our throats, anything
for a tide in our bodies.
Anything for the ocean.

Robin Becker

## *Birch Trees*

From a distance, they are the perfect sentences
we have been reaching for
most of our lives.
They are like the dead

who remember, coming into a room,
how the room grew large
to accommodate
great feeling.

Today in the rain
pale bark unwinds like tiny white flags
and I think of how people
unwrap one another

over a long time and how they learn
the patience to live
alongside the dead who will not speak
and will not go away.

Marc Harshman

## *Listening and Telling*

An old tree, wobbly with yellow fruit.
A scattering of rain,
a steady hiss and patter.
To listen, and see:
the mailbox silver and clean on its old post,
the flowers there bent, their pink lace
broken and crutched on the green netting of weeds,
the hollow rippling with the rising smoke of cool rain.
It takes everything I have to tell you this.
Skill and craft—what are they?
They are nothing, nothing I understand tonight.
The green dollars sitting in the lump of my wallet
sit with me in this cold room. They are awful.
Awful their purpose behind the impossible events
that return from the world of headlines and leaders,
congressmen and briefings.

Bananas and coffee in fluorescent aisles, oil
from sun-lit lands of armies and subterfuge—
what is it they whisper about this green paper,
about the *desaparacidos,* about "linkage?"
And what do I know
but questions and the names of places and people
I'll never see and that there are secrets
and that the secrets are not good:
the rows of steel silos buried in electric earth,
the files of paper notes buried in procedure,
the cold ciphers about bombs and germs and money.
My friends will tell me yes, yes, but not quite,
you're spelling it out all too large.

This is not the place, and my facts not quite straight—
but does it matter, D'Aubbison or Duarte, Hussein or Rafsanjani,
    Republican

or Democrat? Does it matter, really?
The tv will still hum on at six, what can I say?
What do I need? Tell me. Tell someone.
Ten thousand families in the town north
locked to their tv, believing,
believing it all, believing what money tells
others to tell them, others like themselves
believing it's all right since
the right reward of work in a right country
is just this believing itself.

The ground was dry. The rain burned when it began.
I was in the pasture, the blue ironweed nodding, surrounding
me when the shower settled in.
Even then I knew the soldiers would have been killing you,
the old people in their funny hats,
the children crumpled in piles like dolls, the mothers,
the fathers, ears and breasts, and oh all, all the horror.
Outside, the black finery of trees on the western hill,
these under the cool glow of gold pouring into night.
I continue. Tell me it makes a difference,
this listening, this telling everything,
this late light thinning on these comfortable hills.

Honor Moore

## from *Spuyten Duyvil*

**9**

Because he is afraid and powerful
he lives encircled by water.

We hold her as she dies, turn the chairs
to face each other. We breathe with her

as her child is born, let him
cry in the dark as he mourns her death.

When we don't have what we need,
we use what is nearest. One day he

swims the moat to explore the place
which confuses him. There is food when

he reaches the lit house, and stars
hang from the towering branches

of ancient trees. We must learn to rest
when we are tired. Every morning

the sun rises. Every spring green
returns to the cold climates. Bathe

with her, stand with her in her house
smiling as she shows you the

new wood. If their anger frightens you,
try to understand their grief. If you can't

understand what they say, watch
how they move. It's thunder. She

is young. Tell her the truth. He is near
ninety. Help him cross the street. It's

thunder. Reach for my hand, I will
let you go. It's raining. If you

visit, we will walk down through the fields
and I will show you the river.

Nazim Hikmet

## *On Living*

**I**

Living is no laughing matter:
    you must live with great seriousness
        like a squirrel, for example—
I mean without looking for something beyond and above living,
        I mean living must be your whole occupation.
Living is no laughing matter:
        you must take it seriously,
        so much so and to such a degree
    that, for example, your hands tied behind your back,
            your back to the wall,
    or else in a laboratory
        in your white coat and safety glasses,
        you can die for people—
even for people whose faces you've never seen,
even though you know living
        is the most real, the most beautiful thing.
I mean, you must take living so seriously
    that even at seventy, for example, you'll plant olive trees—
    and not for your children, either,
    but because although you fear death you don't believe it,
    because living, I mean, weighs heavier.

## II

Let's say we're seriously ill, need surgery—
which is to say we might not get up
      from the white table.
Even though it's impossible not to feel sad
      about going a little too soon,
we'll still laugh at the jokes being told,
we'll look out the window to see if it's raining,
or still wait anxiously
      for the latest newscast . . .
Let's say we're at the front—
      for something worth fighting for, say.
There, in the first offensive, on that very day,
     we might fall on our face, dead.
We'll know this with a curious anger,
   but we'll still worry ourselves to death
   about the outcome of the war, which could last years.
Let's say we're in prison
and close to fifty,
and we have eighteen more years, say,
     before the iron doors will open.
We'll still live with the outside,
with its people and animals, struggle and wind—
     I mean with the outside beyond the walls.
I mean, however and wherever we are,
  we must live as if we will never die.

## III

This earth will grow cold,
a star among stars
                   and one of the smallest,
a gilded mote on blue velvet—
                   I mean *this*, our great earth.
This earth will grow cold one day,
not like a block of ice
or a dead cloud even
but like an empty walnut it will roll along
                   in pitch-black space . . .
You must grieve for this right now
—you have to feel this sorrow now—
for the world must be loved this much
                   if you're going to say "I lived" . . .

*February 1948*

*translated by Randy Blasing*
*and Mutlu Konuk*

*VIII*

Alice Walker

## *Be Nobody's Darling*

Be nobody's darling;
Be an outcast.
Take the contradictions
Of your life
And wrap around
You like a shawl,
To parry stones
To keep you warm.

Watch the people succumb
To madness
With ample cheer;
Let them look askance at you
And you askance reply.

Be an outcast;
Be pleased to walk alone
(Uncool)
Or line the crowded
River beds
With other impetuous
Fools.

Make a merry gathering
On the bank
Where thousands perished
For brave hurt words
They said.

Be nobody's darling;
Be an outcast.
Qualified to live
Among your dead.

Jeff Oaks

## *Determination*

Among the feathers and grass
the flies dance all day
over the sparrow pulled apart
and scattered in our front lawn.

I am determined not to say
"if only I'd come here earlier . . . "
It would spoil the dancing
I am determined to call transformation.

I am determined not to hate
the cat when he comes in tonight
and lies down beside me.
And, later, when he does come in,

a little dried blood on his chin,
I say good things:  how quick
he must be to catch a bird,
how patient and quiet, how tired

he must be, the bird having fought
him terribly for its life, all
it has, all it had,
even as I have, even as I would.

Morton Marcus

## *The Cell*

Through a microscope
I saw a cell
in a drop of water
spread radiant-edged
in one direction
rather than several others:
sliding, creeping—
a robe, it seemed,
with a soul inside.
Then it twitched,
the cell twitched,
a movement
no more than a wink
yet, in reality,
a kick more violent
than a galaxy shuddering—
and suddenly bigbacked,
the cell wrenched in two:
a seam made visible,
an agony of edges
crawling away
from each other,
like continents
heaving apart,
and *Brother,* I murmured
to each new cell, *Brother.*

To this I bear witness.
I was twelve.
The wonder filled
both my eyes,
although only one eye
saw it, because now
both eyes were brothers,

because now both hands
were friends
who worked together
in the fields, and my feet
an inseparable pair
likely to dance off
in any direction.

At twenty I was shown
how the brain
flies apart like two hands
thrown wide in rapture
under the impact
of a government issue
.45. The man
who demonstrated this
looked nothing like me,
although we were dressed
in the same uniform and spoke
the same language,
and *Brother,* I murmured
to him, *Brother.*
And *Brother,* I murmured
to the boy whose head
had just come apart
and in whose face
I recognized my own.

It is to this dichotomy
that I bear witness—
the cells on one hand,
the brain flying apart
on the other, a separation
comparable to the pulling apart
of continents, of galaxies.
And because I choose the cell
rather than the pistol,
I have lined up with all those
whom the government issue .45

is aimed at, a revolutionary
without politics
in a line with my hands, my feet,
my heart; with my brain
that so easily flies apart;
in line with my brothers
and sisters
as we advance by twos
toward an ark still hidden
by trees and mist.

You will say this is simple,
too simple; that a man my age
should know that one cell
is often inferior to another;
that all cells are not equal;
that just as with bees,
there are worker cells
and management cells
and corporate board cells;
that the crowds of cells
were promised nothing,
have the right to nothing,
and can live comfortable,
decent lives on nothing.

But it's too late.
I've thrown in my lot
with the cells,
with their inalienable,
dignified movement,
their procession toward
all those inalienable things
brothers and sisters
want for their families.
I have chosen this
because the cell chooses
one direction over another,

just as the man behind the gun
chooses to pull the trigger.

Do you understand? Communist
has nothing to do with it.
Neither does Capitalist,
Fascist or Democrat.
It is either the groping
brotherhood of the cell
or the oiled impact
crouching in the .45.

For this choice, each of us
bears witness for the other.

Allen Ginsberg

## *Cosmopolitan Greetings*

*To Struga Festival Golden Wreath Laureates & International Bards*
*    1986*

Stand up against governments, against God.

Stay irresponsible.

Say only what we know & imagine.

Absolutes are Coercion.

Change is absolute.

Ordinary mind includes eternal perceptions.

Observe what's vivid.

Notice what you notice.

Catch yourself thinking.

Vividness is self-selecting.

If we don't show anyone, we're free to write anything.

Remember the future.

Freedom costs little in the U.S.

Advise only myself.

Don't drink yourself to death.

Two molecules clanking against each other require an observer to become scientific data.

The measuring instrument determines the appearance of the phenomenal world (after Einstein).

The universe is subjective.

Walt Whitman celebrated Person.

We are observer, measuring instrument, eye, subject, Person.

Universe is Person.

Inside skull is vast as outside skull.

Who's there in between thoughts?

Mind is outer space.

What do we say to ourselves in bed in the dark, making no sound?

"First thought, best thought."

Mind is shapely, Art is shapely.

Maximum information, minimum number of syllables.

Syntax condensed, sound is solid.

Intense fragments of spoken idiom, best.

Move with rhythm, roll with vowels.

Consonants around vowels make sense.

Savor vowels, appreciate consonants.

Subject is known by what she sees.

Others can measure their vision by what we see.

Candor ends paranoia.

*Boulder, Colorado*
*Kral Majales*
*June 25, 1986*

Judith Vollmer

## *Hold Still*

On the evening of the summer solstice
a hot breeze blows up Forbes Avenue
and the Towers Dorms jut like orange
dayglo popsicles. Suddenly a kid
strolls from around a corner
wearing something between under-
pants & a bathing suit
and he walks by us singing

SEE ME
FEEL ME
TOUCH ME
BLOW ME

He sings to the cop
lighting a cigarette
and to us. We've just heard
that once again Pittsburgh has voted
"Stairway to Heaven" the number one song
of all time, and the last radio caller
lives in Norvelt, Pennsylvania,
the town EleaNOR RooseVELT designed:

Give people an idea
Give people tools and
the country can rebuild itself.
Give each family six acres
each lot a house, coop, grape arbor.
The paper said sign up next week
and the unemployed miners came from Kecksburg,
Weltytown, became carpenters in a month.

A month ago on Pennsylvania Avenue
across from the White House
I saw an old woman washing her clothes
in a fountain. She pulled blouses & rags
from her bag, and now and then she looked up
at the great house where Capital reporters stood
on the lawn under klieg lights breathing
white balloons of moisture, waiting for the signal
to begin talking to the nation.
I saw her exhaustion and thought of Whitman
approaching the hospital tents on the long road,
marching, not wanting to enter one more tent
to take the cool cloths to the boys' faces
but he stood still and did.
You can hear the country listening for something.
Stand with friends at the office or in front of
a class or tv and watch one student stand
in front of a tank and hold off 17 tanks
behind it and imagine holding a moment
a whole country can hold

                              *


I touched the name of Stanislaw Drodz.
I fingered every arc & square of it.
Then I found Steve Martino.
I don't know if you're the Steve Martino
I knew—I don't know if you're the boy I knew
but I touched your name at the black wall in D.C.
in the rain while kids on tour slid by me
on the black marble sidewalk in new hightops.
The sidewalk was made for rain sliding and I'd heard
that unpredictable things happen at the wall.
People find cousins, brothers, sons
by some electromagnetic force pulling them
into the wall, though it looks, as others
have said, like a mirror no one gets inside.
I was pulled by Steve that way

251

when we played Guns of Navarone, Korea Vet,
any game that let us fall down onto the grass
or onto couches in our cellars on Saturdays
while our mothers did the wash. Igloos we built
during the big snows of the Fifties, like damp
cellars, were bunkers where we hoarded surplus
jackets & canteens, grenades & helmets too big
for our heads but perfect for sitting on
protecting our asses from mines & scorpions

where no bomb had ever dropped
but where the mills lay along the riversides
and even now you can hear
something that sounds like voices asking
for your voices. My grandmother would say
these are the voices of the Madonna of the Streets.
She has a face you might know, a plain face with
large bones & a crooked hairline.
She might remind you of someone you passed once
but remembered when you stood in a doorwell of your
office building leaving one world
where the touch of the city's air
moistens the eyes, and another
where the air at your table or desk
protects your secret thoughts.

The cop has carefully guided the singing boy onto a bus.
This is another lucky evening for us.
If I stand still enough I begin to think of beautiful movement
& Pavlova's explanation, in her old age,
of the urgency of learning to dance:

"One was a leaf, or a bud or a flower petal
. . . whatever the occasion demanded."

Susan A. Carlsen

## *Changing Places*

We haven't had a chance to change things.
There is all this noise
And yesterday, children on bicycles.
I'm too weary to weep,
Don't ask that,
That's how the tangling comes,
I start believing in things.

We haven't changed places.
There's a place there
In a square.
I multiplied a few growing things
And the piano's tuned, only
Now, we're trying to break up the box,
How it's lasted so long,
That box there, in the corner.
Blue keeps pouring out of it,
Tearing the edges of things.

We're placed.
We're placed here in window.
If you pass,
See us.
We'll leave the light on.
Curtains open.
Come on a rainy day.
We won't open the door.
We don't hear any more.
Stand outside
The window and watch.
We keep asking you to dream.

Kathe Davis

## *Kumbha Thoughts*

Ohio's water has a funnier
history than most:
burning, dead;
a lake the size of a sea
with nothing that lives on air in it;
the Cuyahoga in flames,
shocking people all over
who mostly decided not to move
to Ohio, where they gun
down their own young,
burn their rivers, kill their lake,
collect the whole country's trash.

But water heals quicker than we do,
better: fish breathe in Erie now.
And a few years ago
my kid and I went
canoeing on the Cuyahoga.
The little river in flood tide,
we went tearing down
at a speed neither of us
knew anything about
how to handle,
inexpert mother,
son learning to know
his parents only apart.
We took water, nearly capsized, grazed
upturned roots, shrieked, were scared
and happy, and the river
didn't burn.

Marc Kaminsky

## *Every Year*

### The Pastor

A great river runs through Hiroshima
and every year
we bring lanterns
inscribed with the names of the family dead
and light them and set them afloat—
lanterns
that carry the dead
vows of the living who will never forget

them and the way they died—
and for miles
the full breadth of the river is one
mass of flames.

Rosaly DeMaios Roffman

## *While It Has You*

hang onto pain

as it moves
down, way down

a single gypsy bead
on a black chain

rail against it
put it in your mouth
tape it to the wall
down, way down

Then let it
tattoo your chest

become a bright bird

with wings that move
when you're without
good clothing

like outdoor roses

remember, you can't
wash away this bird

this angel for stirrings
of roses, your worry bead
turned sparrow—but walk

it says walk
tall and uncovered
that bird

flying those roses
from down, way down

Christina Pacosz

## *Isis Again*

**1**

Black marble sinking
into the earth, the blade
of a shovel turning
death's deep furrow,
the names of these dead,
abundant, but finite;
yours among them.

Eyes scan the list
on panel 33 W, searching
for you, surrounded by so many
brothers, cousins, husbands, lovers—
and then
my finger insists
on pointing the way—
53 . . . 54 . . . 55 . . . 56 . . . 57
and *there you are,* I whisper,

carved in marble and I am
rubbing the letters of your name,
the rarest of cloth covering
well loved skin, the precious
metal of you set in stone
and look
at the good company you keep.

And I am kneeling
and weeping, weeping, kneeling
like women everywhere,
fingering your name
in that country of the dead
where I am, black mirror

where I weep, dark,
diffuse mirror where
I am weeping.
You are two decades gone
to the land of the dead
and only here at the ebony gate

am I allowed to kneel
and follow, weep and touch
what remains: *Anthony A Koster,*
after our grandfather, Tony
to my Tina. Two children,
cousins, one dark, one fair.

A chopper throttles the air,
grim irony, evil throb
and pulse of a heart gone awry,
the swelling music of failure—
*there are no words.*


2

A crow calls. Sound is returned
to us. The world ready
for resurrection
in a blade of grass.

The deep chest breath
of a horse behind me
and I turn thinking
of nothing but you,
how life is bringing
you back.

I wipe my tears into the letters
of your name and when I walk away
I am able to look back
without falling.

**3**

A child wearing a blue jacket
points with her shoe to
the note I've left

and her mother kneels
to read my words to you,
to her.

Yusef Komunyakaa

## *Facing It*

My black face fades,
hiding inside the black granite.
I said I wouldn't,
dammit: No tears.
I'm stone. I'm flesh.
My clouded reflection eyes me
like a bird of prey, the profile of night
slanted against morning. I turn
this way—the stone lets me go.
I turn that way—I'm inside
the Vietnam Veterans Memorial
again, depending on the light
to make a difference.
I go down the 58,022 names,
half-expecting to find
my own in letters like smoke.
I touch the name Andrew Johnson;
I see the booby trap's white flash.
Names shimmer on a woman's blouse
but when she walks away
the names stay on the wall.
Brushstrokes flash, a red bird's
wings cutting across my stare.
The sky. A plane in the sky.
A white vet's image floats
closer to me, then his pale eyes
look through mine. I'm a window.
He's lost his right arm
inside the stone. In the black mirror
a woman's trying to erase names:
No, she's brushing a boy's hair.

# *Thanks*

Thanks for the tree
between me & a sniper's bullet.
I don't know what made the grass
sway seconds before the Viet Cong
raised his soundless rifle.
Some voice always followed,
telling me which foot
to put down first.
Thanks for deflecting the ricochet
against that anarchy of dusk.
I was back in San Francisco
wrapped up in a woman's wild colors,
causing some dark bird's love call
to be shattered by daylight
when my hands reached up
& pulled a branch away
from my face. Thanks
for the vague white flower
that pointed to the gleaming metal
reflecting how it is to be broken
like mist over the grass,
as we played some deadly
game for blind gods.
What made me spot the monarch
writhing on a single thread
tied to a farmer's gate,
holding the day together
like an unfingered guitar string,
is beyond me. Maybe the hills
grew weary & leaned a little in the heat.
Again, thanks for the dud
hand grenade tossed at my feet
outside Chu Lai. I'm still
falling through its silence.
I don't know why the intrepid
sun touched the bayonet,

but I know that something
stood among those lost trees
& moved only when I moved.

Tom Crawford

## *The Heart*

The heart, we tell ourselves, is a pump
like any other.
Some things are just true: the fist
we are asked to tighten
brings up the large vein.
How much grief is enough?
Old Mrs. Vorhees
standing on swollen legs
on the front porch
waving at us, believe it or not,
with a red handkerchief. Now she's dead.
I don't know why we won't listen.
If someone holds up a sign which says,
"You're next," we all look around
for the unlucky one.
Aren't we numbered among the chosen,
what's measurable? The walk to the gate
before boarding. The solitary ride home.

Dick Bakken

## *Going into Moonlight*

I didn't intend
to walk the old road

at midnight
but there I was, surprised

to see my faint shadow
on the dirt. I looked up to that

open moon coming down through
all the mist. A few more steps and there

lay my shadow across a jack rabbit
dead on the road.

I whispered
and reached and there waited

my shadow beneath
as I lifted from the earth the jack by those

silver ears. From beyond
the silhouetted hills, lightning

kept on washing up.
I love

that I couldn't
hear the night wings that passed before

my upturned throat. Only the muffled
roll of thunder far

from the other
side. I swung the jack

high away
into darkness while the next flashes

outlined us. And when I stepped forward, night
misting my face, the shadow

came with me.

Maxine Kumin

## *The Poets' Garden*

After the first revolution
the poets were busier than
cabbage moths in the garden.
They praised the new nation,
the rice paddies, the rumps of the peasants
raised skyward as they planted,
the new children who would grow up to be literate,
have electricity, running water,
almost enough to eat.
They praised the factories
that belonged to everyone,
the bolts of black cloth
and the shimmering orange tractors
that ran like heavy-footed dragons
over the earth.

After the counterrevolution
the poets were excommunicated.
They were farmed out as swineherds.
They cleaned privies.
They swept the aisles of factories.
They learned to make light bulbs and fertilizers
and little by little they mastered
the gray art of ambiguity.
Out of the long and complex grasses
of their feelings they learned
to plait meanings into metaphor.
It was heavy weather.

After the next revolution
it rained melancholy, it is still raining
in the poets' garden. But they are planting
and busy white moths flutter
at random along the orderly rows,

a trillion eggs in their ovipositors
waiting to hatch into green loopers
with fearsome jaws.

Tess Gallagher

## *As If He Were Free*

*for Salman*

Shahid so beautifully brown he is silk
and brown into his brown eyes until
his brown is Krishna-blue. We eat
fiery Brahman lamb—no garlic, no
onions, and lean our elbows onto cushions
until our girlhoods come out because
the threats are elsewhere tonight and
a little silliness with friends is stamina, is
tenacity of the right benevolence when
the time comes, and it does.

For when we talk of Salman we sit upright
and I prepare to listen to the paper
my Kashmiri friend will deliver in the language
of reason before a mostly Western
audience. "It's not entirely
favorable," he cautions, knowing I've spoken
only days ago with Salman, whose hiding
clothes us now in watchfulness and hoping,
an emergence that has freshened the invisible
gates of our words with wounds to the general soul,
when soul is the word for believing the many ways
to die stupidly even without an afterlife, even
with the great quietness of inner sanctity
which questions its gods and is a peasant
with me when Shahid's voice
falls still in the white room, calm in its fluttering and
settling of doves.

No matter these cautionings and positionings of intellect
which choose gingerly among
the defensible objections to what can not be undone—

269

no matter. We are girls again and true
and one of the girls says, "But the thing
not to forget is that he behaved *as if*
he were free." That word "free" heightened always
by its shadow-self of suffering—"Mandela free!"
we say, and if we were only children
when he was taken into the ghost-life that made him live
forever, we are children twice to clap our hands
in joy at his release.

Freedom that is always late because its gliding
attracts the cage, attracts
hindrance as punctuation to its soaring. Freedom—
for sake of which rooms should instantly cloud
with doves when the talk turns murderous. I don't
understand life on earth.
In my girl-soul's mind, I don't understand.

Outside as I write this, the chainsaw I was raised with
drowns gull-light on the harbor where
accounts of riots in Bombay in 1921 will only now
arrive—two "European boys" killing doves, sacred
doves of the mosques, and the sign of the sacred larger
than even rage in the streets or the falling
stock market. The sign melded to its aliveness, not
imagined. "Over doves?" I hear the longshoremen,
incredulous on the docks. "Doves," someone whispers.

The Star of David singes raw the pitiful grass of
Jewish lawns in 1967 in Meridian, Mississippi
where my first love learns to fly jets on the way
to Vietnam, and I look hard into that red dirt.
I still know what it means:  my country still
my country, but lost to me
in malice and ignorance and greed.

At dusk the roar of the chainsaws dies down,
and we pull on our girlhoods, our dovehoods, and go out
to speak in the twin wildernesses

of reason and unreason, in which there is the story of
those eighteenth century birds blinded with
hot needles to make them sing day long, night long and
by candlelight. Or the untelling of the trained doves
who ate cumin from Muhammad's ear.
So that this time one refuses to eat and deposits instead
a strange, wild seed which is already eaten, already
gliding everywhere. And a darkness falls over our cage
the better to hear the *raga* Shahid has
begun to sing, chromatically pure and lonely, no need for key
or harmony, just notes in ascent and descent, each felt
in its individual halo, and for piquancy
an occasional tone added which does not belong, offered

in the blue tatters of the poet.

Gerald Stern

## *Lucky Life*

Lucky life isn't one long string of horrors
and there are moments of peace, and pleasure, as I lie in between the
    blows.
Lucky I don't have to wake up in Phillipsburg, New Jersey,
on the hill overlooking Union Square or the hill overlooking
Kuebler Brewery or the hill overlooking SS. Philip and James
but have my own hills and my own vistas to come back to.

Each year I go down to the island I add
one more year to the darkness;
and though I sit up with my dear friends
trying to separate the one year from the other,
this one from the last, that one from the former,
another from another,
after a while they all get lumped together,
the year we walked to Holgate,
the year our shoes got washed away,
the year it rained,
the year my tooth brought misery to us all.

This year was a crisis. I knew it when we pulled
the car onto the sand and looked for the key.
I knew it when we walked up the outside steps
and opened the hot icebox and began the struggle
with swollen drawers and I knew it when we laid out
the sheets and separated the clothes into piles
and I knew it when we made our first rush onto
the beach and I knew it when we finally sat
on the porch with coffee cups shaking in our hands.

My dream is I'm walking through Phillipsburg, New Jersey,
and I'm lost on South Main Street. I am trying to tell,
by memory, which statue of Christopher Columbus
I have to look for, the one with him slumped over

and lost in weariness or the one with him
vaguely guiding the way with a cross and globe in
one hand and a compass in the other.
My dream is I'm in the Eagle Hotel on Chamber Street
sitting at the oak bar, listening to two
obese veterans discussing Hawaii in 1942,
and reading the funny signs over the honey locust.
My dream is I sleep upstairs over the honey locust
and sit on the side porch overlooking the same culvert
with a whole new set of friends, mostly old and humorless.

Dear waves, what will you do for me this year?
Will you drown out my scream?
Will you let me rise through the fog?
Will you fill me with that old salt feeling?
Will you let me take my long steps in the cold sand?
Will you let me lie on the white bedspread and study
the black clouds with the blue holes in them?
Will you let me see the rusty trees and the old monoplanes one more
        year?
Will you still let me draw my sacred figures
and move the kites and the birds around with my dark mind?

Lucky life is like this. Lucky there is an ocean to come to.
Lucky you can judge yourself in this water.
Lucky the waves are cold enough to wash out the meanness.
Lucky you can be purified over and over again.
Lucky there is the same cleanliness for everyone.
Lucky life is like that. Lucky life. Oh lucky life.
Oh lucky lucky life. Lucky life.

Jane Cooper

## *The Flashboat*

**1**

A high deck. Blue skies overhead. White distance.
The wind on my tongue. A day of days. From the shore a churchbell
    clangs.
Below me the grinding of floes: tiny families huddled together
earth-colored. Let me explain, the ice is cracking free.
They were cut off unawares. From the shore a churchbell clangs.
When the ice breaks up it is spring. No
comfort, no comfort.

**2**

And here is that part of my dream I would like to forget. The purser is
at his desk, he is leaning toward me out of his seat, he is my torturer
who assumes we think alike. Again and again he questions me as to
which national boundaries I plan to cross. *Are you a political activist?*
*No, I'm a teacher.* But already the last villagers have been swept out to
sea. We are cruising north of the Arctic Circle. Without haste he locks
my passport away in his breast pocket. Was I wrong to declare myself
innocent?

**3**

(I did not protest. I spoke nothing but the truth. I never spoke of that
girl who kneeled by her skyscraper window, falling without a sound
through the New York City night.)

**4**

Now it's our turn. Three a.m.
and the Queen Mary is sinking.
All is bustle—but in grays. Red lanterns crawl here and there.
The crew makes ready the boats. One near me, broad but shallow,
looks safe, women are urged, the captain will be in charge.
Far down now:  a trough. A smaller dory rocks
in and out of our lights; black fists grip the oars.
Room only for six—we will
all need to row.
For a moment I hesitate, worrying about my defective blood.
A rope ladder drops over. My voice with its crunch of bone
wakes me: *I choose*
*the flashboat!*
                       work,
                              the starry waters

Maggie Anderson

## *Art in America*

Three of us, two poets and one painter,
drive out into clear autumn weather
to gather in some harvest
from the roadside stands
where pumpkins are piled up
like huge orange marbles in the sun
and the gray Hubbard squash
are disguised as blue toy tops among
blueberries and jugs of apple cider.
We have to make our choices,
as in art, calculate the risk
of making them too ordinary, pale,
like a pool ball hit too thin
because we get afraid
when the table's so alive.
We also risk bravado
(too many pumpkins, or too large)
and, since nothing's ever free,
we might have to put things back.
But today, we think we'll
get it right because
we're not alone
and we're laughing,
arguing a bit,
examining the vegetables,
making up our minds, and
saying how we think we might
believe in the perfection
of communities of artists,
the common work among us.
What one of us does not get said,
the others will.

Jean Valentine

## *After Elegies*

Almost two years now I've been sleeping,
a hand on a table that was in a kitchen.

Five or six times you have come by
the window; as if I'd been on a bus

sleeping through the Northwest, waking up,
seeing old villages pass in your face,

sleeping. A doctor and his wife,
a doctor too, are in the kitchen
area, wide awake. We notice things
differently:  a child's handprint in a clay plate,
a geranium, aluminum
balconies rail to rail, the car horns of a wedding,

blurs of children in white. *LIFE* shots
of other children.    Fire to paper; black

faces, judge faces, Asian faces; flat
earth      your face      fern      coal

Paul Zimmer

## *How Birds Should Die*

Not like hailstones
ricocheting off concrete
nor vaporized through
jets nor drubbed
against windshields
not in flocks
plunged down into
cold sea by
sudden weather no
please no but
like stricken cherubim
spreading on winds
their tiny engines
suddenly taken out
by small pains
they sigh and
float down on
sunlit updrafts
drifting through treetops
to tumble gently
onto the moss

Craig Paulenich

## *Night Sauna*

Druids planted circles of stones
to trace the domed flight of stars,
roofed dolmens humped like sleeping bears.
One afternoon we pulled scores
from the shivering earth,
the wheelbarrow rumbling wildly downhill,
the sweet smell of things exhumed.
We stacked them again and again.
In the slow kinship of their kind,
they squat patiently,
steady as the weighted path of orbits or lives,
hugging each other in shared strength,
filling with heat.

It is good to be naked with friends,
cradled by darkness,
the first great explosion
dimly recalled in flesh,
the glowing soapstone's sear.
We laugh, stay together
as long as possible, then scatter
beneath the heavy curve of holly branches,
dip hot, white bodies
and stand alone, steaming
like stars.

Stanley Plumly

## *Cedar Waxwing on Scarlet Firethorn*

*for John Jones*

To start again with something beautiful,
and natural, the waxwing first on one
foot, then the other, holding the berry
against the moment like a drop of blood—
red-wing-tipped, yellow at the tip of the
tail, the head sleek, crested, fin or arrow,
turning now, swallowing. Or any bird
that turns, as by instruction, its small, dark
head, disinterested, toward the future; flies
into the massive tangle of the trees, slick.
The visual glide of the detail blurs.

The good gun flowering in the mouth is done,
like swallowing the sword or eating fire,
the carnival trick we could take back if
we wanted. When I was told suicide
meant the soul stayed with the body locked in
the ground I knew it was wrong, that each bird
could be anyone in the afterlife,
alive, on wing. Like this one, which lets its
thin lisp of a song go out into
the future, then follows, into the wood-
land understory, into its voice, gone.

But to look down the long shaft of the air,
the whole healing silence of the air, fire
and thorn, where we want to be, on the edge
of the advantage, the abrupt green edge
between the flowering pyracantha and
the winded, open field, before the trees—
to be alive in secret, this is what
we wanted, and here, as when we die what

280

lives is fluted on the air—a whistle,
then the wing—even our desire to die,
to swallow fire, disappear, be nothing.

The body fills with light, and in the mind
the white oak of the table, the ladder
stiffness of the chair, the dried-out paper
on the wall fly back into the vein and
branching of the leaf—flare like the waxwings,
whose moment seems to fill the scarlet hedge.
From the window, at a distance, just more
trees against the sky, and in the distance
after that everything is possible.
We are in a room with all the loved ones,
who, when they answer, have the power of song.

Joy Harjo

## *Eagle Poem*

To pray you open your whole self
To sky, to earth, to sun, to moon
To one whole voice that is you.
And know there is more
That you can't see, can't hear,
Can't know except in moments
Steadily growing, and in languages
That aren't always sound but other
Circles of motion.
Like eagle that Sunday morning
Over Salt River. Circled in blue sky
In wind, swept our hearts clean
With sacred wings.
We see you, see ourselves and know
That we must take the utmost care
And kindness in all things.
Breathe in, knowing we are made of
All this, and breathe, knowing
We are truly blessed because we
Were born, and die soon within a
True circle of motion,
Like eagle rounding out the morning
Inside us.
We pray that it will be done
In beauty.
In beauty.

William Stafford

## *If Only*

If only the wind moved outside, and all else waited,
and at our house nothing moved inside,
and I heard the fumbling air—where could I hide
our pictures and souvenirs, the worn out
clothes we saved, and letters from all the dead?

Afraid even now, I listen. The lock still holds
but the first air touches our door where the whispers came.
I roll up my worthless, priceless pack,
turn with one long reverent look,
and go tumbling downwind calling the names.

# Contributors

MAGGIE ANDERSON is the author of four books of poetry, most recently *Cold Comfort* and *A Space Filled With Moving*, and the editor of Louise McNeill's *Hill Daughter*. One of the organizers of "A Gathering of Poets," she teaches in the English Department at Kent State University.

BILL ARTHRELL, who was indicted as a member of the Kent 25, was arrested twelve times for his political activism in the 1960s and 1970s. He has been an apple picker in Sweden, a movie extra in Hong Kong, and the editor of *Heart's Cargo*.

DICK BAKKEN, author of *Here I Am* and *How to Eat Corn*, resigned his tenured professorship in English at Portland State University in the period following the Kent State and Jackson State shootings to dedicate his "full life energies to poetry."

JAN BEATTY won the Pablo Neruda Prize for Poetry in 1990 and a Pennsylvania Council on the Arts Grant in 1991. She teaches at the University of Pittsburgh.

ROBIN BECKER, poetry editor for *The Women's Review of Books*, is the author of *Backtalk* and *Giacometti's Dog*. She teaches in The Writing Program at Massachusetts Institute of Technology and was a Visiting Poet at Kent State University in Spring 1992.

TOM BECKETT edited and published *The Difficulties* and is the author of eight volumes of poetry, including *Invisible Aria* and *What is a Mouth*.

MARVIN BELL is the author of eight books of poetry, the most recent being *Iris of Creation*, a collection of essays and a poetic collaboration with William Stafford. He lives in Iowa City, where he is on the faculty of the Writers' Workshop, and in Port Townsend, Washington.

JAMES BERTOLINO is the author of seven volumes of poetry, including *Terminal Placebos* and *First Credo*. He is also poetry editor for *In Context: A Quarterly of Humane Sustainable Culture* and teaches at Western Washington University.

ANGELA BILIA, born in Thessaloniki, Greece, received her undergraduate degree from Aristotelean University in 1985. She is finishing her doctorate in English at Kent State University.

RANDY BLASING is the author of *Light Years*, *To Continue* and *The Particles*. He and his wife Mutlu Konuk are the translators of Nazim Hikmet's *Things I Didn't Know I Loved*.

285

ARIEL BLOCH, author of *A Chrestomathy of Modern Literary Arabic,* was born in Germany and taught there before joining the faculty at the University of California at Berkeley.

CHANA BLOCH is the author of *The Secrets of the Tribe* and *The Past Keeps Changing* and translations of Yehuda Amichai and Dahlia Ravikovitch. She teaches at Mills College.

DANIEL BOURNE, editor of *Artful Dodge,* spent 1985–87 in Poland on a Fulbright translating younger poets. He edited the Polish section in an anthology of Eastern European poetry to be published by Fairleigh Dickinson University Press. Bourne teaches at The College of Wooster.

BERTOLT BRECHT was one of this century's greatest playwrights. His major works are *A Man's a Man, The Threepenny Opera, Galileo,* and *Mother Courage and Her Children.*

JAMES BROUGHTON has been a poet and filmmaker for more than four decades. His books include *A Long Undressing: Collected Poems: 1949–1969* and *Special Deliveries.* His films include *The Bed* and *Testament.*

MICHAEL DENNIS BROWNE is the author of four collections of poetry, the most recent being *You Won't Remember This,* and is the librettist for *Harmoonia,* an opera for children, and *As a River of Light,* a musical drama based on the Gospel of Luke.

JOSEPH BRUCHAC is a storyteller and poet from Greenfield Center, New York. Following his 1965 graduation from Cornell University, he spent three years teaching as a volunteer in Africa.

ERNEST BRYLL, currently the Polish ambassador to Ireland, is the author of twenty-four books of poetry and fifteen plays. He has been literary director of the Polish Theater in Warsaw and director of the Polish Cultural Institute in London.

JEANNE BRYNER, winner of the 1990 and 1991 Stan and Tom Wick Poetry Scholarships, is an English major in Kent State University's Honors College.

LEASA BURTON, poetry editor for *The Pennsylvania Review,* is a graduate student at the University of Pittsburgh. She received a 1990 Associated Writing Program Intro Award.

SUSAN A. CARLSEN received an M.F.A. from the University of Oregon, has published in *Black Warrior Review,* and was an organizer for "A Forest Gathering of Poets" in Eugene, Oregon, in 1991.

286

MARY M. CHADBOURNE, vice-president of the Institute for Environmental Education, co-founded the Poets' League of Greater Cleveland's "Poetry: Mirror of the Arts" series.

KELLY CHERRY is the author of *Natural Theology, My Life and Dr. Joyce Brothers,* and *The Exiled Heart.* Her tenth book is scheduled for publication next year by the Louisiana State University Press. She teaches at the University of Wisconsin at Madison.

AMY CLAMPITT was born and brought up in rural Iowa, graduated from Grinnell College, and lives in New York City. She is the author of four collections of poetry and of *Predecessors, Et Cetera,* a collection of essays.

KEVIN CLARK is the author of *Granting the Wolf* and *Widow Under a New Moon.* Presently working on a volume of poems about men and violence, he teaches creative writing and modern poetry at California Polytechnic State University at San Luis Obispo.

LUCILLE CLIFTON is the author of *Good Times, An Ordinary Woman, Generations: A Memoir,* and several children's books.

JANE COOPER is the author of *The Weather of Six Mornings, Maps and Windows,* and *Scaffolding: New and Selected Poems.* She recently retired from Sarah Lawrence College, where she taught for many years.

SOPHIE CRAWFORD received an M.F.A. in Creative Writing from the University of Oregon and works with memory-impaired adults in Portland. Her poems have appeared in *Soundings East, Fireweed, Cold-Drill,* and *Big Rain.*

TOM CRAWFORD is the author of *It It Weren't for Trees.* He lives in Oregon and recently spen a year at Sichuan International University in Chongqing, China.

JIM DANIELS is the author of *Places/Everyone* and *Punching Out.* He teaches at Carnegie-Mellon University.

KATE DANIELS is the author of two volumes of poetry, *The White Wave* and *The Niobe Poems,* and is the editor of *The Selected Poems of Muriel Rukeyser.* She lives in Durham, North Carolina.

KATHE DAVIS, one of the organizers of "A Gathering of Poets," teaches English at Kent State University. She has had poems in *Coventry Reader* and *The Time of Your Life,* and she has a recent article on John Berryman in *Conrad Aiken: A Priest of Consciousness.*

287

TOI DERRICOTTE was born in Hamtramck, Michigan, studied special education at Wayne State University, and earned an M.A. in English from New York University. She is the author of *The Empress of Death House* and *Natural Birth*. She has been a MacDowell Fellow and currently teaches at the University of Pittsburgh.

DIANE DI PRIMA is the author of *Revolutionary Letters, The Calculus of Variation,* and *Pieces of a Song*. She teaches at the San Francisco Institute of Magical and Healing Arts, which she co-founded in 1983.

PATRICIA DOBLER, director of the Women's Creative Writing Center at Carlow College in Pittsburgh, is the author of *Talking to Strangers* and *UXB*.

SHARON DOUBIAGO won a 1991 Oregon Book Award for Poetry for *Psyche Drives The Coast, Poems 1975–87*. She is also the author of *Hard Country, The Book of Seeing With One's Own Eyes,* and *South America Mi Hija*.

RITA DOVE won the 1987 Pulitzer Prize for her third book of poems, *Thomas and Beulah*. She is the author of the novel *Through the Ivory Gate* and the verse drama *The Darker Face of the Earth*. She teaches at the University of Virginia.

LYNN EMANUEL is the author of *Hotel Fiesta* and *The Dig*, which won the National Poetry Series Award. She teaches at the University of Pittsburgh.

JULIE FAY is the author of *Portraits of Women*. Currently she is writing a novel set in seventeenth-century New England. She teaches at East Carolina University.

EDWARD FIELD, editor of the anthology *A Geography of Poets,* is the author of *Stand Up, Friend, With Me, Variety Photoplays,* and *New and Selected Poems: From the Book of My Life*.

ANNE FRYDMAN, who teaches at The Writing Seminars at Johns Hopkins University, has translated three works of Sergei Dovlatov. Since receiving her doctorate at Columbia University in 1978, she has written on Anton Chekhov's short stories and currently is writing on the last years of Isaac Babel.

TESS GALLAGHER is the author of *Amplitude: New and Selected Poems* and *Portable Kisses*. She has written the introduction to *Carver Country,* a volume of photographs by Bob Adelman which documents the life and work of her late husband, Raymond Carver.

ALEX GILDZEN is Curator of Special Collections and Archives at the Kent State University Libraries, where he has cataloged the papers of James Broughton, Joseph Chaikin, and Jean-Claude van Itallie. He is the author of *The Avalanche of Time: Selected Poems 1964–1984* and *Postcard Memoirs*.

288

ALLEN GINSBERG is the author of *Howl and Other Poems, Kaddish and Other Poems,* and *Collected Poems 1947–1980.* Transcripts of his talks at Kent State University are included in *Allen Verbatim: Lectures on Poetry, Politics, Consciousness.*

PATRICIA GOEDICKE is the author of *The Tongues We Speak,* a 1990 "New York Times Notable Book of the Year," and *Paul Bunyan's Bearskin.* She teaches in the Creative Writing Program at the University of Montana.

DONALD HALL is the author of eight books of poetry, from *Exiles and Marriages,* which won the 1955 Lamont Prize, through *The Happy Man.* He co-edited the landmark anthology *New Poets of England and America.*

JOSEPH HANSEN is the author of a collection of poems, *One Foot in the Boat,* and the Dave Brandstetter mystery novels. "Vocalese," a musical setting of four of his poems by Richard Rodney Bennett, was first performed in 1983.

YVONNE MOORE HARDENBROOK was an education writer while teaching in the Columbus, Ohio, schools in the 1960s. She is the author of *saying enough* and is included in the anthology *A Wider Giving: Women Writing After a Long Silence.*

JOY HARJO is the author of four books of poetry, the most recent being *In Mad Love and War.* She is the winner of the 1990 American Indian Distinguished Achievement Award and the 1991 William Carlos Williams Award from the Poetry Society of America. She teaches creative writing at the University of New Mexico.

MARC HARSHMAN is the author of a book of poems, *Turning Out the Stones,* and of several books for children, including *A Little Excitement* and *Snow Company.* He lives in Moundsville, West Virginia.

DAVID HASSLER grew up in Kent, Ohio. He graduated from Cornell University and did graduate work at Kent State University.

DONALD HASSLER, coordinator of Graduate Studies in English at Kent State University, is the author of *Comic Tones in Science Fiction* and studies of Isaac Asimov and Hal Clement.

NAZIM HIKMET, who died in 1963, was a poet, playwright, and novelist whose advocacy of communism resulted in frequent imprisonments in Turkey before he fled to the Soviet Union in 1951.

BRENDA HILLMAN is the author of *White Dress, Fortress, Death Tractates,* and *Bright Existence.* She teaches at St. Mary's College in Moraga, California.

TIFF HOLLAND was one of the organizers of "A Gathering of Poets." A 1989 graduate of Kent State University, she won a Tom and Stan Wick Poetry Scholarship and the Donna Zurava Memorial Award.

BROOKE HORVATH is an editor for *The Review of Contemporary Fiction* and for *Athelon: The Journal of Sport Literature*. He teaches at the Stark Campus of Kent State University.

CHRISTOPHER HOWELL, a veteran of both the Vietnam conflict and the protests against it, is the author of *Sweet Afton*. He teaches at Emporia State University in Kansas.

DAVID IGNATOW is the author of *Poems, 1934–1969, New and Collected Poems, 1970–1985,* and *The One in the Many: A Poet's Memoirs*. He lives in East Hampton, New York.

LAWSON FUSAO INADA writes books for children and teaches English at Southern Oregon State College.

LOWELL JAEGER is the author of *War on War* and *Hope Against Hope*. He lives in Bigfork, Montana.

LORI JAKIELA, editor of *The Pennsylvania Review*, is a graduate student at the University of Pittsburgh. Her poems have appeared in *Poem, West Branch,* and *Yarrow.*

LAWRENCE JOSEPH is the author of *Shouting At No One,* which won the Starrett Poetry Prize, and *Curriculum Vitae*. A National Endowment for the Arts poetry fellow, he teaches law at St. John's University School of Law.

MARC KAMINSKY is the author of six volumes of poetry, including *The Road from Hiroshima* and *Target Populations*. He has been a writer-in-residence with the Open Theater, The Talking Band and Ballad Theater, and is a psychotherapist in private practice in Brooklyn.

GALWAY KINNELL won the Pulitzer Prize for Poetry in 1983 for *Selected Poems.*

YUSEF KOMUNYAKAA, 1992 Holloway Poet at Berkeley, is the author of *Magic City* and *Neon Vernacular: New and Selected Poems 1977–89*. He teaches creative writing and African American literature at Indiana University.

KAREN KOVACIK, a recent recipient of an Individual Artists Fellowship from the Ohio Arts Council, is a poetry fellow at the University of Wisconsin's Institute for Creative Writing.

MORT KRAHLING is the author of *Swiss Cross Mystery* and *Caught in the Glow*. He tends bar and works in an antiquarian bookstore next door to Brady's Cafe in Kent, Ohio.

MAXINE KUMIN won the Pulitzer Prize for Poetry in 1973 for *Up Country*. She is also the author of *In Deep: Country Essays*, *Nurture: Poems*, and the novel *The Passions of Uxport*. She lives in Warner, New Hampshire.

JACOB LEED is the author of *In Japan: Poems and Drawings* and editor of *The Computer & Literary Style: Introductory Essays and Studies*. A retired Kent State University English professor, he lives in Cambridge, Massachusetts.

DENISE LEVERTOV is the author of many collections, including *Overland to the Islands*, *The Jacob's Ladder*, *The Sorrow Dance*, and *Collected Earlier Poems*. Her essays are collected in *The Poet in the World*.

M. L. LIEBLER is the author of six books, including *Breaking the Voodoo* and *Deliver Me*, and co-editor of *Save the Frescoes That Are Us: A Detroit Tribute to Jack Kerouac*. President of The Poetry Resource Center of Michigan, he teaches at Wayne State University.

JUDY LINDBERG, winner of the Academy of American Poets Prize, has published poems in *Artpaper*, *The Madison Review*, *Southern Poetry Review*, and *Spoon River Quarterly*. She teaches at Pennsylvania State University.

MICHAEL MCCAFFERTY, a Kent State University graduate, is a writer and artist whose "Earthworks/Bodyworks" were done in the Pacific Northwest. He is Exhibition Designer for the Seattle Art Museum.

IRENE MCKINNEY is the author of *The Girl With The Stone In Her Lap*, *Quick Fire and Slow Fire*, and *Six O'Clock Mine Report*. She teaches at West Virginia Wesleyan University.

LOUISE MCNEILL, poet laureate of West Virginia, is the author of five books of poetry, including *Paradox Hill*, *Elderberry Flood*, and *Hill Daughter*, and a memoir, *The Milkweed Ladies*. She lives in Malden, West Virginia.

PETER MAKUCK, editor of *Tar River Poetry*, is the author of *Breaking and Entering* and *The Sunken Lightship*. A graduate of Kent State University, he teaches at East Carolina University.

OSIP MANDELSTAM, who is believed to have died in a Siberian prison camp in 1938, was a Russian poet, novelist, and critic whose anti-Stalin writings made him an enemy of the state.

MORTON MARCUS is the author of six books of poems, the most recent being *Pages From A Scrapbook of Immigrants: A Journey in Poems* and a novel, *The Brezhnev Memo*. His work has appeared in sixty anthologies and more than two hundred magazines. He teaches at Cabrillo College in Aptos, California.

WILLIAM MATTHEWS is the author of *Ruining the New Road, Rising and Falling,* and *A Happy Childhood.* He co-edited the magazine *Lillabulero.* He teaches at the City College of New York.

PAUL METCALF, winner of the 1987 Morton Dauwen Zabel Award from the American Academy and Institute of Arts and Letters, is the author of twenty-one books, including *Genoa, I-57,* and *Araminta and the Coyotes.*

THOMAS MEYER is the author of *The Bang Book, The Umbrellas of Aesculapius, Sappho's Raft,* and *Tom Writes This For Robert To Read.* He lives in North Carolina and the Yorkshire Dales.

ELIZABETH MIHALY, a graduate assistant in the English department at Kent State University, received the department's 1990 Donna Zurava Memorial Award for a portfolio of her poems.

CONNIE MONSON was a student of Patricia Goedicke at the University of Montana, where she received an M.F.A.

HONOR MOORE, author of *Memoir,* lives in Kent, Connecticut, where she is completing a biography of her grandmother, the painter Margarett Sargent.

TODD MOORE, editor of *Road/House,* is the author of *The Man in the Black Chevrolet, The Dark and Bloody Ground,* and *Dillinger.*

JILL MOSES received an M.F.A. in creative writing from the University of Oregon, where she was assistant poetry editor of *Northwest Review.* She teaches at Thomas Nelson Community College in Virginia.

LISEL MUELLER was born in Germany and came to the United States as a child. Her books include *Dependencies, The Private Life,* and *The Need to Hold Still.*

JEFF OAK received an M.F.A. from the University of Pittsburgh, where he now teaches.

ED OCHESTER is the writing program director at the University of Pittsburgh, editor of the University of Pittsburgh Press Poetry Series, and president of Associated Writing Programs. He is the author of *Miracle Mile* and *Changing the Name to Ochester.*

SHARON OLDS, who holds a Ph.D. from Columbia University, won the National Book Critics Circle Award in 1985 for *The Dead and the Living*. She teaches at New York University.

ALICIA OSTRIKER is the author of seven books of poetry, the most recent being *Green Age*, and a critical work, *Stealing the Language: The Emergence of Women's Poetry in America*. She teaches at Rutgers University.

CHRISTINA PACOSZ is the author of four books, including *Notes From The Red Zone* and *This Is Not A Place To Sing*. She lives in Delta Junction, Alaska, where she teaches children with learning disabilities.

KARL PATTEN, 1989 Poet of the Year at the Millay Colony, co-edits *West Branch* and teaches at Bucknell University.

CRAIG PAULENICH, co-editor of *Beneath a Single Moon: Buddhism in Contemporary American Poetry*, teaches English at the Salem Campus of Kent State University.

JOHN PERREAULT, poet, performance artist, and art critic, is the author of *Camouflage, Luck,* and *Harry* and is editor of *Elephant* and *Only Prose*. He is senior curator at the American Craft Museum in New York City.

JUDITH RACHEL PLATZ is the author of *Tending the Dark*. Her poems and reviews have appeared in *The Greenfield Review, Haight Ashbury Review,* and *Milkweed Chronicle*. She teaches at the University of New England in Biddeford, Maine.

STANLEY PLUMLY, who edited *The Ohio Review* while teaching at Ohio University, is the author of several books of poetry, including *In the Outer Dark, Giraffe, Out-of-the-Body Travel,* and *Boy on the Step*.

FRANK POLITE, a vocational rehabilitation counselor for the state of Ohio, has had work in the anthologies *A Geography of Poets* and *A Cleveland Sampler*. He lives in Youngstown.

STEVE POSTI is a 1990 graduate of Kent State University. He lives in Jupiter, Florida.

DEBORAH PURSIFULL, winner of a 1988 American Academy of Poets Award, is the author of *The Truck Poems* and *The Beauty of Falling*. Former editor of *The Pennsylvania Review*, she lives in Pittsburgh.

MAJ RAGAIN was born in Olney, Illinois, and recently lived in Thessaloniki, Greece. He is the author of *Gail Ray's Drowning in Olney Poem* and co-author of *Northfield Thistledown Making Book*.

JAMES RAGAN, director of the Master of Professional Writing Program at the University of Southern California, is the author of three books of poetry and the plays *Saints* and *Commedia*. He co-edited *Yevgeny Yevtushenko: Collected Poems, 1952–1990*.

DAHLIA RAVIKOVITCH is Israel's best-known woman poet. She has published six volumes of poetry in Hebrew, a book of short stories, and two books of children's verse. Her most recent collection in English, *The Window: New and Selected Poems*, was translated and edited by Chana and Ariel Bloch.

JUDITH ROCHE teaches through the Artist in Residence program for Washington State and helps organize the annual Bumbershout Festival in Seattle.

ROSALY DEMAIOS ROFFMAN is the author of *Facing the Angels* and co-editor of *Life on the Line*, an anthology on healing with words. She teaches mythology and creative writing at Indiana University of Pennsylvania.

CHARLES ROSSITER is producer and host of the television program *Poetry Motel* and first vice-president of the National Association for Poetry Therapy. He is the author of *Thirds* and *The Man With Two Day's Stubble*.

VERN RUTSALA is the author of *Ruined Cities, Walking Home from the Icehouse, The Journey Begins*, and *The Window*. He teaches at Lewis and Clark College.

MAXINE SCATES is the author of *Toluca Street* and is a former poetry editor of *Northwest Review*. She lives in Eugene, Oregon.

GARY SCOTT, a graduate of Kent State University, lives in Warren, Pennsylvania, where he works as an optician.

RICHARD SHELTON is the author of *Selected Poems: 1969–1982, The Bus to Veracruz,* and *Hohokam*. His nonfiction work, *Going Back to Bisbee*, won the Western States Award. He is a Regents Professor at the University of Arizona, Tucson.

DAVID SHEVIN, co-editor of *A Red Shadow of Steel Mills,* is the author of *Growl* and *The Discovery of Fire*. He teaches at Tiffin University.

DOROTA SOBIESKA is a native of Poland currently doing graduate work in the English Department at Kent State University.

JOHN SOLLERS has taught high school English for twenty years in his native Idaho and seven years in Oregon, where he now lives. His work is included in *A Centennial Anthology of Idaho Poets*.

WILLIAM STAFFORD is the author of *Things That Happen Where There Aren't Any People, Stories That Could Be True: New and Collected Poems,* and *Traveling Through the Dark,* which won the National Book Award. He lives in Lake Oswego, Oregon.

ANN STANFORD, who died in 1987, was the author of eight books of poetry, including *The Weathercock* and *In Mediterranean Air.* She taught for twenty-five years at California State University, Northridge.

KEVIN STEIN is the author of *James Wright: The Poetry of a Grown Man* and the collection of poems *A Circus of Want.* He teaches at Bradley University in Illinois.

GERALD STERN is the author of *Lucky Life, Leaving Another Kingdom: Selected Poems,* and *Bread Without Sugar.* He teaches at the Writers' Workshop at the University of Iowa.

LUCIEN STRYK is the author of *Collected Poems, Of Pen and Ink and Paper Scraps,* and *Triumph of the Sparrow: Zen Poems of Shinkichi Takahashi.* He teaches at Northern Illinois University.

WILLIAM STUDEBAKER is the author of *The Rat Lady at the Company Dump* and *Backtracking: Ancient Art in Southern Idaho.* He teaches at the College of Southern Idaho.

SHINKICHI TAKAHASHI was a dadaist poet in Japan in the 1920s before beginning training in Zen. His books of poetry include *Solar Eclipse, Rain Cloud, The Body,* and *Sparrow;* he is also the author of *Essays on Zen Study* and *Poetry and Zen.*

DANIEL THOMPSON, a graduate of Kent State University, was arrested nineteen times during his tenure as a civil rights organizer with Martin Luther King, Jr. He is the author of *Famous in the Neighborhood.*

BILL TREMBLAY is the author of *Crying in the Cheap Seats, The Anarchist Heart, Second Sun: New & Selected Poems,* and *Duhamel.* He teaches at Colorado State University.

TONY TRIGILIO received a B.S. from Kent State University, where he researched and wrote articles on the May 4 shooting for the campus newspaper and yearbook. He received an M.A. from Northeastern University and returned to Kent for doctoral work.

JEAN VALENTINE is the author of five collections of poetry, the most recent being *Home. Deep. Blue. : New & Selected Poems.* She teaches at Sarah Lawrence College and lives in New York City.

295

JEAN-CLAUDE VAN ITALLIE is a writer and antinuclear activist. His plays include *America Hurrah, The Serpent, The Traveller,* and *Ancient Boys.* He also has adapted the major plays of Anton Chekhov for the English-language stage.

JUDITH VOLLMER won the 1990 Brittingham Prize in Poetry for her first collection, *Level Green.* She teaches at the University of Pittsburgh at Greensburg and co-edits *5 A.M.*

ALICE WALKER is the author of *Revolutionary Petunias and Other Poems, Langston Hughes: American Poet,* and *The Color Purple,* which won the Pulitzer Prize for Fiction in 1983. She was writer-in-residence at Jackson State College the year before the shootings.

MICHAEL WATERS is the author of five books of poetry, including *Anniversary of the Air* and *Bountiful.* He teaches at Salisbury State University in Maryland.

LYNN WIKLE has published poems in *Poetry Northwest* and other small journals. She lives and teaches on the central Oregon coast.

C. K. WILLIAMS is the author of *Tar* and *A Dream of Mind.* He lives in Paris and teaches part of the year at George Mason University.

JONATHAN WILLIAMS is a poet and publisher whose Jargon Society has published many of the century's major poets. He is the author of *An Ear in Bartram's Tree, The Loco Logodaedalist in Situ,* and *Elite/Elate Poems.*

SANDRA WILLIAMS has published poems in *The Chadakoin Review, Fusion West, Hubbub,* and *The Threepenny Review.* She teaches at Mt. Hood Community College in Oregon, where she coordinates the Mountain Writers Series.

ALAN WILLIAMSON is the author of *Presence* and *The Muse of Distance.* He teaches at the University of California at Davis.

C. D. WRIGHT has published six collections of poetry, the most recent being *String Light.* She is the winner of the 1986 Witter Bynner Prize for Poetry and the 1989 Whiting Writer's Award. Co-editor of Lost Roads Publishers, she teaches at Brown University.

PAUL ZIMMER, a graduate of Kent State University, is the author of *Ribs of Death, The Zimmer Poems, Family Reunion,* and *Great Bird of Love.* He is the director of the University of Iowa Press.

# Acknowledgments

Maggie Anderson: "Art in America" and "Heart Fire" are reprinted from *Cold Comfort*, by Maggie Anderson, by permission of the University of Pittsburgh Press. © 1986 by Maggie Anderson.

Bill Arthrell: The excerpt from *Kent 25* is printed with the permission of the poet.

Dick Bakken: "Going into Moonlight" was originally published in a limited edition by Carrington Press, Maple Valley, WA, 1989; reprinted in *Plowshares* 16, 1 (Spring/Summer 1990) and in *Magee Park Poets Anthology 1991*, Carlsbad, CA, 1990. It is reprinted with the permission of the poet.

Jan Beatty: "Asking the Dead for Help" is printed with the permission of the poet.

Robin Becker: "Birch Trees" is reprinted from *Giacometti's Dog*, by Robin Becker, by permission of the University of Pittsburgh Press. © 1990 by Robin Becker.

Tom Beckett: "Specific Nouns," © 1988 by Tom Beckett, from *Separations* (Generator Press, 1988). Reprinted by permission of publisher John Byrum and the poet.

Marvin Bell: "Green" is printed with the permission of the poet.

James Bertolino: "Five Views of the New History" and "The American" from *First Credo*. Copyright © 1986 by *Quarterly Review of Literature* Poetry Series, Vol. XXVI. Reprinted by permission of *Quarterly Review of Literature* Poetry Series.

Angela Bilia: "Red Carnations" is printed with the permission of the poet.

Chana Bloch: "Rising to Meet It" first appeared in *Poetry* (April 1990). It is reprinted with permission of the poet.

Daniel Bourne: "The Language of the Dead" first appeared in *Poetry East*. It is reprinted with permission of the poet.

James Broughton: "For a Gathering of Poets" is printed with permission of the poet.

Michael Dennis Browne: "May Four" first appeared in *The Southern California Anthology*. It is reprinted by permission of the poet and *The Southern California Anthology*.

299

Joseph Hansen: "To Jeffrey Miller" first appeared in *Beyond Baroque*, Vol. 1, No. 3 (August 1970). It is reprinted with permission of the publisher George Drury Smith and the poet.

Yvonne Moore Hardenbrook: "History Lesson" first appeared in *Whalebone and Royal Blood* (Sophia Books, 1985); reprinted in the anthology *A Wider Giving: Women Writing After A Long Silence,* edited by Sondra Zeidenstein (Chicory Blue Press, 795 East Street North, Goshen CT 06756).

Joy Harjo: "Eagle Poem" is reprinted from *In Mad Love and War*, © 1990 by Joy Harjo (Wesleyan University Press), by permission of University Press of New England.

Marc Harshman: "Listening and Telling" first appeared in *5 AM,* 3 (1989). It is reprinted with permission of the poet and editor Judith Vollmer.

David Hassler: "May 1990" is printed with permission of the poet.

Donald Hassler: "May 4, 1970" first appeared in *Ball State University Forum* 11, 3 (Summer 1970). It is reprinted with permission of the editor and the poet.

Nazim Hikmet: "On Living," translated by Mutlu Konuk and Randy Blasing, is printed with permission of Persea Books, Inc., and the translators.

Brenda Hillman: "White Deer" is printed with permission of the poet.

Tiff Holland: "May 4, 1990" is printed with permission of the poet.

Brooke Horvath: "A Matter of Trees," copyright © 1991 by The Antioch Review, Inc., first appeared in *The Antioch Review* 49, 2 (Spring 1991). Reprinted by permission of the Editors.

Christopher Howell: "Liberty & Ten Years of Return" originally appeared in *The Antioch Review*; reprinted in *Sea Change* (Seattle, 1985), and in *Carrying The Darkness: American Indochina—The Poetry of the Vietnam War* (Avon, 1985). "A Reminder to the Current President" originally appeared in *Hubbub;* reprinted in above volumes. Both poems reprinted with permission of the poet.

David Ignatow: "Soldier" is reprinted from *Rescue the Dead*, © 1968 by David Ignatow (Wesleyan University Press) by permission of University Press of New England.

Lawson Fusao Inada: "From Ancient to Present: Homage to Kent State" is printed with permission of the poet.

Lowell Jaeger: "The War At Home" reproduced by permission of Utah State University Press from *War On War*, Lowell Jaeger (Logan: Utah State University Press, 1988), 31–32. Not for further reproduction.

301

Louise McNeill: "The Grave Creek Inscribed Stone" from *Elderberry Flood* (Elderberry Books, 1979) is reprinted with permission of the West Virginia Division of Culture and History. "The Three Suns" is reprinted by permission of the poet, © 1991 by Louise McNeill.

Peter Makuck: "The Commons" copyright © 1982 by Peter Makuck. Reprinted from *Where We Live, Poems by Peter Makuck* with the permission of BOA Editions Ltd., 92 Park Avenue, Brockport NY 14420.

William Matthews: "Why We Are Truly A Nation" appeared in *Ruining the New Road* (Random House, 1970). It is printed with permission of the poet.

Morton Marcus: "The Cell" is printed with permission of the poet.

Paul Metcalf: His untitled piece is printed with permission of the author.

Thomas Meyer: "The Desert" from *Fourteen Poems*, copyright 1989 by Thomas Meyer. Reprinted by permission of The French Broad Press, Asheville, N. C.

Elizabeth Mihaly: "May 4th" is printed with permission of the poet.

C. L. Monson: "Kent State" is printed with permission of the poet.

Honor Moore: "Spuyten Duyvil, 9" was published in *Memoir,* Poems by Honor Moore (Chicory Blue Press, 795 East Street North, Goshen CT 06756). © 1988 by Honor Moore. Reprinted with permission of the poet and the publisher.

Todd Moore: "i've never told" is printed with permission of the poet.

Jill Moses: "'Child with a toy hand grenade in Central Park, N.Y.C.'" is printed with permission of the poet.

Lisel Mueller: "Bedtime Story" is reprinted by permission of Louisiana State University Press from *Waving from Shore*, Poems by Lisel Mueller. Copyright © 1979, 1986, 1987, 1988, 1989 by Lisel Mueller.

Jeff Oaks: "Determination" is printed with permission of the poet.

Ed Ochester: "Oh, By the Way" first appeared in *Ploughshares*. The translation of Bertolt Brecht's "On the Infanticide" is reprinted from *Miracle Mile* by permission of Carnegie-Mellon University Press. © 1984 by Ed Ochester.

Sharon Olds: "The Protestor" first appeared in *The Paris Review*. It is reprinted with permission of the poet and *The Paris Review.*

Alicia Ostriker: "Cambodia," from *The Mother/Child Papers* (Momentum Press, 1980); reprinted by Beacon Press, 1986. © Alicia Ostriker. Reprinted with permission of the poet.

304

Judith Vollmer: "Hold Still" first appeared in *Level Green* (University of Wisconsin Press, 1990).

Alice Walker: "Be Nobody's Darling," from *Revolutionary Petunias and Other Poems,* copyright © 1972 by Alice Walker, is reprinted by permission of Harcourt Brace Jovanovich, Inc., and David Higham Associates, London.

Michael Waters: "The Torches" from *Bountiful* (Carnegie-Mellon University Press, 1992), © Michael Waters. It first appeared in *The American Poetry Review* 18, 6 (Nov.-Dec. 1989) and is reprinted with permission of the poet.

Lynn Wikle: "Three Lakes, Wisconsin" is printed with permission of the poet.

C. K. Williams: "In the Heart of the Beast" from *Poems, 1963–1983,* copyright © 1988 by C. K. Williams. Reprinted by permission of Farrar, Straus & Giroux, Inc. and the author.

Jonathan Williams: "the fbi files on" from *Quantulumcumque,* copyright 1991 by Jonathan Williams. Reprinted by permission of The French Broad Press, Asheville, NC.

Sandra Williams: "Learning to Fish" first appeared in *Calapooya Collage* 9 (Summer 1985). It is reprinted with permission of editor Tom Ferte.

Alan Williamson: "Freeze-Frame" is printed with permission of the poet.

C. D. Wright: "The Legend of Hell" is reprinted from *Further Adventures with You* by permission of Carnegie-Mellon University Press. © 1987 by C. D. Wright.

Paul Zimmer: "How Birds Should Die" was published in *Live with Animals* (Ampersand Press) and reprinted in *The Great Bird of Love* (Urbana: University of Illinois Press, 1989), © 1989 by Paul Zimmer. It is reprinted with the permission of the poet and the University of Illinois Press.

# Editors' Note

The editors are grateful to the following for assistance in the completion of the collection: the Kent State University Department of English, Department of Special Collections and Archives, University Libraries and its May 4 Collection, and the Research Council. The editors are also grateful to the following individuals: Nancy Birk, Claire Culleton, Kathe Davis, Virginia Dunn, Elizabeth French, David Hassler, Tiff Holland, Dimitris Karageorgiou, Sanford Marovitz, Peter Oresick, Judith Rachel Platz, and Maj Ragain.

# Author Index

308

309

*A Gathering of Poets* was composed in Times Roman on an NEC PowerMate computer using PageMaker 4.0 software by Raymond A. Craig; with Linotronic output at 1270 dots per inch by Southern California PrintCorp; printed by sheet-fed offset on 60-pound Glatfelter Natural Smooth acid-free stock, Smyth sewn and bound over binder's boards in Holliston Kingston Natural cloth with Rainbow Antique endpapers, also adhesive bound with paper covers printed in two colors on 12-point stock and film laminated by Braun-Brumfield, Inc.; text designed by Raymond A. Craig; paper cover and case designed by Will Underwood; and published by *The Kent State University Press,* Kent, Ohio 44242.